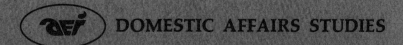

GOVERNMENT-MANDATED PRICE INCREASES

A Neglected Aspect of Inflation

Murray L. Weidenbaum

GOVERNMENT-MANDATED PRICE INCREASES

GOVERNMENT-MANDATED PRICE INCREASES

PRICE INCREASES

A Neglected Aspect of Inflation

Murray L. Weidenbaum

American Enterprise Institute for Public Policy Research
Washington, D. C.

Murray L. Weidenbaum is director of the Center for the Study of American Business at Washington University in St. Louis, Missouri, and an adjunct scholar at the American Enterprise Institute.

ISBN 0-8447-3151-x

Domestic Affairs Study 28, February 1975

Library of Congress Catalog Card No. 75-841

Printed in the United States of America

CONTENTS

1   INTRODUCTION AND SUMMARY   **1**

2   THE TIP OF THE ICEBERG: FEDERAL INSPECTORS AND REGULATORS   **7**

Varieties of Federal Controls   7
Types of Federal Inspection   8
The Paperwork Burden   12
Impact on Manufacturing Costs   20

3   HIGHER COSTS OF AUTOMOBILES   **23**

The Cost to the Consumer   25
On-the-Job Training Costs for Regulators   28

4   HIGHER COSTS OF CONSUMER PRODUCTS   **31**

The Impact on Consumers   32
The Impact on Business   34
The Power of Government Regulation   35
Labels and Labeling   38
Outlook   40

5   HIGHER COSTS OF INDUSTRIAL PRODUCTION   **43**

Ladders, Exits, and Other Trivia   45
Lack of a Sense of Proportion   47
Is the Objective to Punish or to Improve
    Conditions?   50
Cost of Government Controls   51
Announcement Effect   54
Outlook   55

6   HIGHER COSTS OF GOVERNMENT PURCHASES   57

Historical Development of Required Social
   Responsibility   57
Disadvantages and Shortcomings   60
Adverse Effects on Defense Production   63

7   HIGHER COSTS OF PERSONNEL   67

Federally Mandated Fringe Benefits   67
The Federal Government and Personnel Practices   70
Future Trends—Employee Testing   73
Future Trends—Employee Housing   75
Concluding Note   75

8   HIGHER INTEREST RATES   77

Effects on Total Saving and Investment   78
Effects on Sectors of the Economy   79
Growth of Federal Credit Programs   80
Relation to Government Controls   84
Summary   86

9   THE COSTS OF CONFLICTING GOVERNMENT
     OBJECTIVES: WHICH "GOOD" IS BETTER?   87

Regulating Restrooms: A Case of Separate
   But Equal   88
Who Will Regulate the Regulators?   90
Conclusion   94

10   THE GOVERNMENTAL PRESENCE IN BUSINESS
      DECISION MAKING   97

A Second Managerial Revolution   98
The Various Costs of Federal Regulation   101
The Changing Structure of the Economy   105
A New Approach to Business-Government
   Relations   107

1
INTRODUCTION AND SUMMARY

> The dollars that private enterprises and individuals are required to spend for environmental and other purposes are no less a drain on output because they come from private pockets than they would be if they came directly from government coffers.
>
> Milton Friedman

As the American public is learning to its dismay, there are many ways in which government actions can cause or worsen inflation. Large budget deficits and excessively easy monetary policy are usually cited as the two major culprits, and quite properly. Yet, there is a third, less obvious—and hence more insidious—way in which government can worsen the already severe inflationary pressures affecting the American economy.

That third way is for the government to require actions in the private sector which increase the costs of production and hence raise the prices of the products and services which are sold to the public. As shown in Chapter 3, for example, the price of the typical new 1974 passenger automobile is about $320 higher than it would have been in the absence of federally mandated safety and environmental requirements. Attention needs to be focused on this third route to inflation for two reasons: (1) the government is constantly embarking on new and expanded programs which raise costs and prices in the private economy and (2) neither government decision makers nor the public recognize the significance of these inflationary effects. Literally, the federal government is continually mandating more inflation via

The diligent efforts of the author's research assistant, James Langenfeld, a graduate student at Washington University, are gratefully acknowledged. Lee Benham of Washington University and Dan Larkins of the American Enterprise Institute provided numerous helpful suggestions. The views expressed are, of course, solely those of the author.

the regulations it promulgates. These actions of course are validated by an accommodating monetary policy.

In theory, the monetary authorities could offset much of the inflationary effects of regulation by attempting to maintain a lower rate of monetary growth. In practice, however, public policy makers, insofar as they see the options clearly, tend to prefer the higher rate of inflation to the additional monetary restraint and the resulting decreases in employment and real output.

Obviously, most of these government actions are not designed to increase prices. Nevertheless, that is their result. In part because of efforts to control the growth of government spending, we have turned increasingly to mechanisms designed to achieve a given national objective—better working conditions, for example, or more nutritious foods—without much expenditure of government funds. The approach emphasizes efforts to influence private decision makers to achieve specific ends. Thus, rather than burden the public treasury with the full cost of cleaning up environmental pollution, we now require private firms to devote additional resources to that purpose. Rather than have the federal government spend large sums to eliminate traffic hazards, we require motorists to purchase vehicles equipped with various safety features that increase the selling price.

At first blush, government imposition of socially desirable requirements on business appears to be an inexpensive way of achieving national objectives: it costs the government nothing and therefore is no burden on the taxpayer. But, on reflection, it can be seen that the public does not escape paying the cost. For example, every time that the Occupational Safety and Health Administration imposes a more costly, albeit safer, method of production, the cost of the resultant product will necessarily tend to rise. Every time that the Consumer Safety Commission imposes a standard which is more costly to attain, some product costs will tend to rise. The same holds true for the activities of the Environmental Protection Agency, the Food and Drug Administration, and so forth.

The point being made here should not be misunderstood. What is at issue is not the worth of the objectives of these agencies. Rather, it is that the public does not get a "free lunch" by imposing public requirements on private industry. Although the costs of government regulation are not borne by the taxpayer directly, in large measure they show up in higher prices of the goods and services that consumers buy. These higher prices, we need to recognize, represent the "hidden tax" which is shifted from the taxpayer to the consumer. Moreover, to the extent that government-mandated requirements impose similar costs on all price categories of a given product (say, automobiles), this hidden tax will tend to be more regressive than the federal income tax. That is, the costs may be a higher relative burden on lower income groups than on higher income groups.

This study does not address the philosophical question of whether government regulation is good or bad. Government regulation is an accepted fact in a modern society. The point being made here is the more modest one that a given regulatory activity generates costs as well as benefits. Hence, consideration of proposals—and they are numerous—to extend the scope of federal regulation should not be limited, as is usually the case, to a recital of the advantages of regulation. Rather, the costs need to be considered also, both those which are tangible and those which may be intangible.

It should be acknowledged that what is taking place in the United States represents not an abrupt departure from an idealized free market economy, but rather the rapid intensification of fairly durable trends of expanding government control over the private sector. In earlier periods, when productivity and living standards were rising rapidly, the nation could more easily afford to applaud the benefits and ignore the costs of regulation. But now the acceleration of federal controls coincides with, and accentuates, a slowdown in productivity growth and in the improvement in real standards of living. Thus, the earlier attitude of tolerance toward controls is no longer economically defensible.

Worthy objectives, such as a cleaner environment and safer products, can be attained without the inflationary impact that regulation brings, and public policy should be revised to this end. But before we turn to this question, we need to examine more closely the phenomenon of government-mandated price increases. It is likely that this unwanted phenomenon will be with us for some time—at least until consumers and their representatives recognize the problem and urge changes in public policy.

As these government-mandated costs begin to visibly exceed the apparent benefits, it can be hoped that public pressures will mount on governmental regulators to moderate the increasingly stringent rules and regulations that they apply. At present, for example, a mislabeled consumer product that is declared an unacceptable hazard often must be destroyed. In the future, the producer or seller perhaps will only be required to relabel it correctly, a far less costly way of achieving the same objective.

Yet, the recent trend is clear—more frequent and more costly governmental regulation of the private sector. Table 1 summarizes

Table 1

EXTENSION OF GOVERNMENT REGULATION OF BUSINESS, 1962–73

Year of Enactment	Name of Law	Purpose and Function
1962	Food and Drug Amendments	Require pretesting of drugs for safety and effectiveness and labeling of drugs by generic names
1963	Equal Pay Act	Eliminates wage differentials based on sex
1964	Civil Rights Act	Creates Equal Employment Opportunity Commission (EEOC) to investigate charges of job discrimination
1965	Cigarette Labeling and Advertising Act	Requires labels on hazards of smoking
1966	Fair Packaging and Labeling Act	Requires producers to state what package contains, how much it contains, and who made the product
1966	Child Protection Act	Bans sale of hazardous toys and articles
1966	Traffic Safety Act	Provides for a coordinated national safety program, including safety standards for motor vehicles
1967	Flammable Fabrics Act	Broadens federal authority to set safety standards for inflammable fabrics, including clothing and household products
1967	Wholesome Meat Act	Offers states federal assistance in establishing interstate inspection system and raised quality standards for imported meat
1967	Age Discrimination in Employment Act	Prohibits job discrimination against individuals aged 40 to 65
1968	Consumer Credit Protection Act (Truth-in-Lending)	Requires full disclosure of terms and conditions of finance charges in credit transactions
1968	Interstate Land Sales Full Disclosure Act	Provides safeguards against unscrupulous practices in interstate land sales
1968	Wholesome Poultry Products Act	Increases protection against impure poultry

Year of Enactment	Name of Law	Purpose and Function
1968	Radiation Control for Health and Safety Act	Provides for mandatory control standards and recall of faulty atomic products
1969	National Environmental Policy Act	Requires environmental impact statements for federal agencies and projects
1970	Public Health Smoking Act	Extends warning about the hazards of cigarette smoking
1970	Amendment to Federal Deposit Insurance Act	Prohibits issuance of unsolicited credit cards. Limits customer's liability in case of loss or theft to $50. Regulates credit bureaus and provides consumers access to files
1970	Securities Investor Protection Act	Provides greater protection for customers of registered brokers and dealers and members of national securities exchanges. Establishes a Securities Investor Protection Corporation, financed by fees on brokerage houses
1970	Poison Prevention Packaging Act	Authorizes establishment of standards for child-resistant packaging of hazardous substances
1970	Clean Air Act Amendments	Provide for setting air quality standards
1970	Occupational Safety and Health Act	Establishes safety and health standards which must be met by employers
1971	Lead-Based Paint Elimination Act	Provides assistance in developing and administering programs to eliminate lead-based paints
1971	Federal Boat Safety Act	Provides for a coordinated national boating safety program
1972	Consumer Product Safety Act	Establishes a commission with power to set safety standards for consumer products and ban those products presenting undue risk of injury
1972	Federal Water Pollution Control Act	Declared a national goal to end the discharge of pollutants into navigable waters by 1985

Table 1 *(continued)*

Year of Enactment	Name of Law	Purpose and Function
1972	Noise Pollution and Control Act	Regulates noise limits of products and transportation vehicles
1972	Equal Employment Opportunity Act	Gives EEOC right to sue employers
1973	Emergency Petroleum Allocation Act	Establishes temporary controls over petroleum
1973	Vocational Rehabilitation Act	Requires federal contractors to take affirmative action on hiring the handicapped

some of the major extensions of this trend in recent years. This monograph is not concerned only with a past trend, however. For example, the desire to increase the federal role in health care while minimizing the burden on the public treasury has led to a variety of proposals to require employers to pay part of the cost of health insurance for their employees and their families. Although these proposals would not directly result in an added burden on the taxpayer, they would increase the cost of doing business and would inevitably lead to higher prices to consumers or in lower wages for employees.

If the trend continues unchecked, the resulting loss in productivity could lead to stagnation in real living standards. Further expansion of government control over private industry is not inevitable, however. Not all controls last forever and the federal government does not adopt every suggestion for increasing government controls over the private sector. For example, in January 1974, the government ended the interest equalization tax on American holdings of foreign stocks and bonds and the controls over direct investments abroad by U.S. corporations. Simultaneously, the Federal Reserve System ended its guidelines limiting lending and investments overseas by U.S. banks and other financial institutions. Further, on April 30, 1974, the legislation authorizing wage and price controls was allowed to expire and the formal wage and price control system was dismantled. Yet it is likely that some vestige of government influence over private price formation will remain. The recently established Council on Wage and Price Stability appears to be in an early stage of its development; it is expected to "jawbone" against large wage and price increases. To a limited extent, the newer controls over energy use are performing some of the functions previously exercised by the wage and price review system.

2

THE TIP OF THE ICEBERG: FEDERAL INSPECTORS AND REGULATORS

> The single most important source of economic waste comes from failure to identify and evaluate what is being given up when we go for something that itself is "good."
>
> Paul W. McCracken

This newer type of government control differs in many ways from the older and more formal regulation by independent commissions, such as the Interstate Commerce Commission, Federal Power Commission, Federal Communications Commission, Securities and Exchange Commission, and Civil Aeronautics Board. Most of those efforts focused on regulating a specific industry—railroads, oil pipelines, television stations, and so forth. The more recent regulatory efforts established by the Congress are not so limited. They cut across virtually every branch of private industry. Environmental controls apply to all companies, as do requirements concerning job safety and occupational health.

Varieties of Federal Controls

Many federal controls do not stand alone, but rather accompany other federal programs. For example, the program of financial assistance to the American merchant marine for the acquisition of new vessels also involves federal determination of which "national defense" features must be incorporated into vessel construction and what kind of record keeping and reporting shall be required.

Increasingly, government procurement contracts spell out not only what contractors must provide to the government, but also how they should go about producing the goods and services. These requirements range from hiring and training minority groups to federally set wage-and-hour standards to favoring depressed areas and small business firms in subcontracting. Federal contractors are required to adhere to energy conservation measures which are voluntary for all other companies. The Vocational Rehabilitation Act of 1973 compels employers with federal contracts over $2,500 to take "affirmative action" to hire handicapped workers. These are only a sampling of the federal requirements which are described in detail in Chapter 6.

The tax collector also serves as regulator or at least a source of strong influence. With the carrot of tax incentives, the federal government tries to induce greater "social responsibility" from the private sector. Specific internal revenue provisions used in this manner include tax credits for hiring certain people and not others, tax deferrals for exports but not for imports, and tax reductions for investing in capital goods but not for current operating expenses. At times the linkage between taxes and controls is very direct and obvious. Thus, in order to qualify for rapid tax amortization of pollution control devices a facility must be certified by both the state and the regional office of the U.S. Environmental Protection Agency.

Types of Federal Inspection

Federal inspectors, an increasingly important physical presence in private industry, are concerned with a growing list of responsibilities. The Supreme Court recently ruled that air pollution inspectors do not need search warrants to enter the property of suspected polluters as long as they do not enter areas closed to the public. The unannounced and warrantless inspections were held not to be in violation of constitutional protections against unreasonable search and seizure.[1] The inspectors of the Labor Department's Occupational Safety and Health Administration (OSHA) can go further. They have "no-knock" power to enter the premises of virtually any business in the United States, without a warrant or even prior announcement, to inspect for health and safety violations. Jail terms are provided in the OSHA law for anyone tipping off a "raid." A recent court test has reaffirmed the right of OSHA compliance inspectors to enter a work site for inspections without so much as a "by your leave." A U.S. district court, acting on the case of a firm which had refused an inspector entry until the company's attorney was present, ruled that the federal agents did not need search warrants to enter workplaces.[2]

---

[1] Air Pollution Variance Board of the State of Colorado v. Western Alfalfa Corporation, 94 S. Ct. 2114 (May 20, 1974).

[2] "Court Upholds 'Free Entry' for OSHA," *Industry Week*, July 15, 1974, p. 9.

The literature on public administration does not emphasize the role of the government official as inspector. Yet this often unwelcome visitor is making his appearances with increasing frequency. As shown in Table 2, the work force of federal regulatory agencies is

Table 2

RISING EMPLOYMENT OF FEDERAL REGULATORY AGENCIES, 1973–75

(fiscal years)

Agency	Number of Persons Employed		
	1973 (actual)	1974 (estimate)	1975 (estimate)
Cost Accounting Standards Board	38	41	41
Federal Energy Administration	—	965	1,040
Office of Telecommunications Policy	57	52	60
Agriculture:			
Animal and Plant Health Inspection Service	13,773	13,970	14,100
Commodity Exchange Authority	156	180	209
Packers and Stockyards Administration	188	190	196
Commerce:			
Office of Foreign Direct Investment	95	90	42
National Bureau of Fire Prevention	—	—	104
Health, Education, and Welfare:			
Food and Drug Administration	6,676	6,351	6,482
Interior:			
Mining Enforcement and Safety Administration	2,298	2,563	2,910
Fuel allocation, oil and gas programs	67	1,200	2,135
Labor:			
Employment Standards Administration	2,399	2,611	2,630
Occupational Safety and Health Administration	1,285	1,605	1,756
Transportation:			
National Highway Traffic Safety Administration	747	779	836
Federal Railway Administration	1,174	1,243	1,312
National Transportation Safety Board	269	265	275

Table 2 *(continued)*

Agency	Number of Persons Employed		
	1973 (actual)	1974 (estimate)	1975 (estimate)
Treasury:			
Bureau of Alcohol, Tobacco and Firearms	3,751	3,672	3,780
Environmental Protection Agency	8,270	9,203	9,203
Civil Aeronautics Board	679	700	713
Consumer Product Safety Commission	579	776	978
Equal Employment Opportunity Commission	1,739	2,252	2,339
Federal Communications Commission	1,750	1,972	1,992
Federal Maritime Commission	282	306	316
Federal Metal and Nonmetallic Mine Safety Board of Review	2	2	2
Federal Power Commission	1,246	1,297	1,337
Federal Trade Commission	1,446	1,560	1,609
Interstate Commerce Commission	1,795	1,870	2,060
Marine Mammals Commission	—	6	11
National Labor Relations Board	2,339	2,454	2,454
Occupational Safety and Health Review Commission	147	188	188
Renegotiation Board	188	200	200
Securities and Exchange Commission	1,579	1,910	1,985
Tariff Commission	302	381	400
Total	55,316	60,854	63,695

Source: *Budget of the United States Government, Fiscal Year 1975,* Appendix.

undergoing a major expansion and is scheduled to exceed 63,000 in fiscal year 1975. The direct cost of these activities to the American taxpayer is, of course, quite substantial and is also growing. In fiscal year 1972 (July 1, 1971 to June 30, 1972), federal spending for the various business inspection and regulatory activities came to $1.3 billion. By fiscal 1974, such spending had increased 46 percent, reaching an annual total of $1.9 billion. For fiscal 1975, the figure is estimated at approximately $2.2 billion (see Table 3).

Yet, these expenditures are only the tip of the iceberg. The major costs resulting from the operations of the growing force of

Table 3

FEDERAL EXPENDITURES FOR BUSINESS REGULATION, 1972–75

(fiscal years, $ millions)

Agency	1972	1973	1974 (esti- mated)	1975 (esti- mated)
Agriculture	280	323	328	349
Health, Education, and Welfare	88	118	140	156
Interior	a	55	116	140
Justice	56	74	105	130
Labor	143	91	132	171
Transportation	128	166	176	204
Treasury	114	189	208	241
Environmental Protection Agency	144	184	247	297
Civil Aeronautics Board	76	86	83	83
Equal Employment Opportunity Commission	21	28	41	53
Federal Communications Commission	28	34	40	45
Interstate Commerce Commission	60	44	38	47
National Labor Relations Board	47	48	56	62
Securities and Exchange Commission	26	30	36	42
Nine other commissions	97	102	154	142
Total	1,308	1,572	1,900	2,162

a not available

Source: *Budget of the U.S. Government,* fiscal years 1974 and 1975; Cost of Living Council data.

federal inspectors and regulators show up in the added expenses of business firms which must comply with their directives. A substantial "inflationary multiplier" must be applied to the direct outlays for federal controls.

The process of federal inspection and regulation gives rise to a variety of added business costs. U.S. Steel Corporation estimates that its superintendents and foremen spent 4,000 man-hours in 1972 guiding inspectors through its coal mines, in addition to the reports and paperwork required. Also, the need for government inspectors has siphoned off experienced supervisory personnel at a time when the coal industry needs many more people with managerial ability.

Consolidation Coal is said to have lost 600 foremen to the ranks of federal inspectors.[3]

The Paperwork Burden

A direct cost imposed on business firms as a result of governmental inspections and controls is the growing paperwork burden, that is, the expensive and time-consuming process of submitting reports, making applications, filling out questionnaires, replying to orders and directives, and appealing in the courts from other rulings and regulatory opinions. As of June 30, 1974, according to the Office of Management and Budget, there were 5,146 different types of approved public-use forms, excluding all tax and banking forms. Individuals and business firms spend over 130 million man-hours a year filling out federal forms.[4]

The extended process of federal control inevitably produces a "regulatory lag," a delay that can run into years and be a severe drag on managerial decision making. For example, 30 percent of the electric utility rate cases decided in 1973 dragged on for more than one year, some of them taking more than two years to be settled.[5] Prior to the 1962 amendments to the food and drug law, the Food and Drug Administration took, on average, seven months to process a new drug application. The more stringent regulation imposed in 1962 has increased the regulatory lag to two-and-one-half years.[6]

Regulatory delay and mountains of paperwork constitute a particularly costly burden for small businesses. A firm employing not more than fifty people is required to fill out as many as seventy-five to eighty different types of forms in the course of one year.[7] The lack of understanding between the regulators and those they regulate is vividly conveyed in the following interchange reported by a small manufacturer who attended a meeting to discuss the paperwork burden. When he was advised to have his staff complete the forms, he

---

[3] "No Easy Out: Coal's Troubles Cloud 'Best Answer' to the Energy Crisis," *Wall Street Journal*, November 21, 1973, p. 24.

[4] Statement of Robert H. Marik, associate director for management and operations, Office of Management and Budget, before the House Committee on Government Operations, 93d Congress, 2d session (September 13, 1974), p. 5.

[5] Murray L. Weidenbaum, *Financing the Electric Utility Industry* (New York: Edison Electric Institute, 1974), Chapter 5.

[6] Sam Peltzman, *Regulation of Pharmaceutical Innovation* (Washington, D. C.: American Enterprise Institute, 1974).

[7] U.S. Congress, Senate, Select Committee on Small Business, *The Federal Paperwork Burden*, 93d Congress, 1st session (1973), p. 2.

replied, "When I attend this meeting the staff is right here with me. It's me." [8]

For a small enterprise that employs seventy-five people, two employees working half time to fill out government forms may not sound particularly burdensome until one considers that the plant's productivity increases for the year might be substantially reduced as a result. In contrast, a plant with 5,000 employees can much more easily afford to employ a staff of ten working full time to meet federal requirements. The larger company can spread the cost of one "non-productive" staff member over the work output of 500 employees.

A small, 5,000-watt radio station in New Hampshire reported that it spent $26.23 just to mail its application for license renewal to the Federal Communications Commission. An Oregon company operating three small television stations reported that its license renewal application weighed forty-five pounds. These small stations apparently were required to fill out the same forms as the multi-million dollar radio and television stations operating in major metropolitan areas. [9]

One small businessman, James Baker, president of Gar-Baker Laboratories in New York City, lamented the long list of government forms his five-man firm must fill out:

(1) Thirty-seven filings on twelve different federal forms, ranging from tax reports to data for the Census Bureau to registration with the Food and Drug Administration;

(2) Twenty-six sets of data for nine different New York state agencies, including employee and tax records, an alcohol permit, and information on disability-benefits insurance; and

(3) Twenty-five forms for twelve different city departments, including a variety of tax records, a chemical permit from the fire department, two refrigerator permits, and one deep-freeze permit. [10]

A large corporation, with about 40,000 employees, reports that it uses 125 file drawers of backup material just to meet federal reporting requirements on personnel. The equivalent of fourteen full-time employees is required to staff this personnel reporting activity. The personnel manager estimates that one-third of his staff could be

[8] Ibid., pp. 3-4.

[9] Ibid., p. 10.

[10] "Smothered in Paper Work—Businessmen Are Fed Up," *U.S. News and World Report*, April 29, 1974, pp. 57-58.

13

eliminated if there were no federal, state or local reporting requirements.[11]

The Federal Trade Commission is now attempting to obtain "line of business" data on the nation's 345 largest corporations. The commission's staff believes that the costs of the program will be "modest in relation to the substantial benefits" which will result from the additional information.[12] This conclusion is reached on the basis of cost estimates from a sample of twenty-five major companies which, on the average, figure the "setting up costs" of providing the new information at $548,000 (see Table 4). Assuming that the $548,000 is representative, this means that the total initial cost of this single report from the 345 companies will be about $190 million. This may be a "modest" sum from the viewpoint of the government, but it is a substantial overhead cost to the companies involved and ultimately will be passed on, in good measure, to the consumer.

In contrast, some of the reporting requirements of the newer federal regulatory agencies may result in a heavier burden on small business. In its first several years of operation, the Occupational Safety and Health Administration, which was established under a law passed in 1970, required virtually all employers to keep three separate records: a log of occupational injuries and illnesses, a supplementary record of each occupational injury or illness, and a summary sheet of injuries and illnesses (OSHA forms 100, 101, and 102, respectively). A supplemental quarterly survey was also required (OSHA forms 102F and 102FF). These had to be kept up to date and accurate, even if an employer had only one employee.[13] How essential this information really was can be judged from OSHA's reaction to recent pending legislation which would have relieved all employers of fifteen or fewer persons from the agency's record keeping and reporting requirements. Suddenly, OSHA determined that employers of seven or fewer persons could be exempted from its paperwork requirements!

The OSHA reports and records, of course, are in addition to the traditional forms required by other federal agencies. To illustrate the problem, the Graymills Corporation, which employed 120 workers in 1972, compiled a list of the forty different government forms which

---

[11] Correspondence with the author, July 17, 1974, St. Louis, Missouri.

[12] U.S. Congress, Senate, Subcommittee on Budgeting, Management, and Expenditures of the Committee on Government Operations, *Hearings on Corporate Disclosure*, 93d Congress, 2d session (1974), p. 924.

[13] U.S. Department of Labor, *What Every Employer Needs to Know About OSHA Record Keeping*, B.L.S. Report No. 412 (revised), 1973, p. 3.

it is required to fill out (see Table 5). Some of these forms must be filled out several times a year and others must be completed for each employee.

Table 4
ESTIMATED START-UP COSTS FOR FTC LINE-OF-BUSINESS REPORTS
(\$ thousands)

Company	Estimated Mean Start-Up Costs
American Metal Climax	75
Anaconda	1,000
Combustion Engineering	100
Crown Zellerbach	100
Deere	1,000
Dow Chemical	400
DuPont	500
Ex-cell-o	350
Exxon	1,000
General Instrument	100
Inland Steel	100
Lear Siegler	400
McGraw-Hill	45
Mobil	500
Nabisco	100
Northrop	300
Outboard Marine	100
R. J. Reynolds	1,000
Singer	500
Standard Oil, California	800
Union Carbide	1,100
U.S. Steel	2,000
Varian Associates	63
Westinghouse	2,000
Westvaco	75
Total	13,708
Mean	548

Source: U.S. Congress, Senate, Subcommittee on Budgeting, Management, and Expenditures of the Committee on Government Operations, *Hearings on Corporate Disclosure,* 93d Congress, 2d session (1974), p. 922.

Table 5

GOVERNMENT FORMS REQUIRED OF
GRAYMILLS CORPORATION

Agency	Form or Subdivision	Form Number
Federal		
Department of Commerce	Census of Manufacturers	MC-35M
Office of Equal Employ-ment Opportunity	Employer Information Report EEO-I	265-41
Federal Trade Commission	Division of Financial Statistics	MG-1
Department of Labor	Log of Occupational Injuries and Illnesses	100
Department of Labor	Supplementary Record of Occupational Injuries and Illnesses	101
Department of Labor	Summary—Occupational Injuries and Illnesses	102
Department of Labor	Wage Developments in Manufacturing	BLS 2675b
Department of Labor	Employee Welfare or Pension Benefit Plan Description	D-1
Department of Labor	Employee Welfare or Pension Benefit Plan Description Amendment	D-1A
Department of Labor	Employee Welfare or Pension Benefit Plan Annual Report	D-2
Department of Labor	Information on Employee Welfare or Pension Benefit Plan Covering Fewer than 100 Participants	D-3
Department of Treasury	Federal Tax Deposits—Withheld Income and FICA Taxes	501
Department of Treasury	Unemployment Taxes	508
Department of Treasury	Employer's Annual Federal Unemployment Tax Return	940
Department of Treasury	Employee's Withholding Exemption Certificate	W-4
Department of Treasury	Reconciliation of Income Tax Withheld from Wages	W-3
Department of Treasury	Report of Wages Payable Under the Federal Insur-ance Contributions Act	941a

Agency	Form or Subdivision	Form Number
Department of Treasury	Return of Employee's Trust Exempt from Tax	990-P
Department of Treasury	U.S. Information Return for the Calendar Year 1971	1099
State of Illinois		
Industrial Commission	Application for Adjustment of Claim—Notice of Disputed Claims and Memorandum of Names and Addresses	None
Industrial Commission	Employer's Report of Compensable Injury	None
Industrial Commission	Memorandum of Names and Addresses for Service of Notices	None
Industrial Commission	Notice of Filing Claim	77
Industrial Commission	Report of Accident	C174
Employment Service	DOL-BES Form	None
Division of Unemployment Compensation	Notice of Possible Ineligibility	UC (III.) Ben-22
Division of Unemployment Compensation	Employer's Contribution Report	UC-3D
Department of Revenue	Retailers' Occupation Tax, Use Tax, County, Municipal Service Occupation and Service Use Tax Return	RR-1A
Department of Revenue	Employee's Illinois Withholding Exemption Certificate	II-W-4
Department of Revenue	Monthly State Income Tax Payment Form	II-501
Department of Revenue	Application for Renewal of Resale Certificate Number	RR-4904
State of California		
Department of Business Taxes	State, Local, and District Sales and Use Tax Return	BT 401C
State of New Jersey		
Division of Taxation	Resale Certificate	SF-3
Division of Taxation	Blanket Exemption Certificate	1786 AC
City of Chicago		
Commission on Human Relations	Contractor Employment Practices Report	None
Metropolitan Sanitary District	Industrial Waste Surcharge Certified Statement	FI-235

Table 5 *(continued)*

Agency	Form or Subdivision	Form Number
City of Chicago (con't.)		
Metropolitan Sanitary District	Report of Exemption Claim or Estimate of Liability for Surcharge	FI-236
Metropolitan Sanitary District	Computation of Initial Estimate of Liability for Surcharge	FI-236A
City of Los Angeles		
Department of Building and Safety	Application and Agreement for Testing Electrical Equipment	B&S E-147
Department of Building and Safety	Application for Approval Labels	B&S R9

Source: U.S. Senate, Subcommittee on Government Regulation of the Select Committee on Small Business, *Hearings on the Federal Paperwork Burden*, 93d Congress, 1st session (1973), Part 1, pp. 124-28.

Filling out these forms may require more educated and hence more expensive workers than are assigned to producing the company's products. A sense of the frustration experienced by the small businessman who is burdened with the growing array of federal forms can be gleaned from a sampling of the correspondence received by the Small Industry Committee of the Illinois Manufacturer's Association:

> The bureaucrats can't seem to comprehend that we out of the government have to work for a living and that these papers detract from our productive time. . . .
>
> I have no argument with the policies of EEOC, OSHA, Corps of Engineers effluent controls, etc. But not enough thought has been put on minimizing unnecessary data and reports, in my opinion. In a small plant of 75 people, we have two men working half time on programs with attendant detailed plans and reports which were not necessary 2-3 years ago. . . .
>
> Our greatest concern is the changing of forms each time they become due. Especially in small businesses where it is necessary for one person to take care of several phases of the work, we find we are having to spend many hours keeping informed of changes made on the forms, and studying all the fine print. . . .[14]

---

[14] U.S. Congress, Senate, Select Committee on Small Business, *Hearings on the Federal Paperwork Burden*, 93d Congress, 1st session (1973), Part I, pp. 122-23.

The U.S. Office of Management and Budget estimates that the reporting burden imposed on American business by the federal government increased by 50 percent between December 1967 and June 1974.[15] Major new programs—occupational safety and health activities, medicare and medicaid, environmental protection regulations, and equal employment opportunity compliance—were the principal sources of the increase (see Table 6).

One of the problems is that government officials review proposed forms from the standpoint of the needs of government rather than from that of the private respondent. The Office of Management and Budget, which has the responsibility for minimizing the paperwork burden resulting from federal requirements, was unable to tell a congressional committee the exact number of forms (or which ones) a typical small business might be required to fill out each year. One method of reducing the mountain of federally mandated paperwork might be to require that a form must be eliminated unless someone in the government actually reads all the information which is submitted!

Table 6

SOURCES OF MAJOR INCREASES IN REPORTING BURDEN ON AMERICAN BUSINESS, DECEMBER 1967–JUNE 1974
(millions of man-hours)

Category	Increase
Occupational safety and health	+ 4.6
Social security (mainly Medicare and Medicaid)	+ 2.7
Manpower programs	+ 1.3
Equal employment opportunity	+ 1.1
Aircraft and airport regulations	+ 1.0
Housing production and mortgage guarantee programs	+ 0.9
Foreign trade documentation	+ 0.7
Environmental protection	+ 0.6
Employment statistics	+ 0.6
Total	+13.5

Source: Statement of Robert H. Marik, associate director for management and operations, Office of Management and Budget, before the House Committee on Government Operations, 93d Congress, 2d session (September 13, 1974), p. 5.

[15] Statement of Marik, pp. 8-9.

The paperwork burden imposed by government regulatory agencies on private industry is likely to expand as the result of recent congressional action. A rider attached to the Alaska pipeline bill (Public Law 93-153) shifted the authority to review proposed questionnaires of federal regulatory commissions from the Office of Management and Budget to the General Accounting Office (GAO). In the process, the power to disapprove unnecessary reports has been converted to the responsibility of merely issuing advisory opinions to the agencies, and the latter now have the final power to decide whether the burdens that a required report imposes on the private sector are necessary. Unlike OMB, GAO cannot now rule on "the necessity of the information." In the past, the value of the data requested was compared to the trouble and cost of gathering it before a questionnaire was approved.

An effort also appears to be underway to shift many government questionnaires from a voluntary to a compulsory basis. At present, an organization's decision to respond to almost all quarterly and monthly surveys by nonregulatory agencies is voluntary. The Bureau of Labor Statistics has urged the Congress to make mandatory as many as ten of its surveys on prices, wages, and employment.[16]

Impact on Manufacturing Costs

Although the paperwork burden may be one of the most bothersome elements attached to federal controls over business, other aspects of regulation can be far more costly. For example, the U.S. Council on Environmental Quality has estimated that the private sector's capital investment requirements for pollution control equipment will come to $112 billion in the decade 1972–81 (see Table 7).

In the popular image, the supporters of tighter pollution controls are the good guys in the white hats, while those who "create" the pollution are the villainous bad guys. Yet, as the environmental regulatory process develops, it seems to be acquiring many of the standard characteristics of any bureaucratic activity. One of these characteristics is preoccupation with the agency's objectives, while ignoring other concerns of the society. The highway builders in the 1950s and early 1960s were attacked, quite properly, for seemingly wanting to convert the American landscape into one vast coast-to-coast cement roadway. Unfortunately, the environmentalists seem to be adopting a similar attitude. An assistant EPA administrator was

---

[16] "Wringing Data Out of Business," *Business Week*, March 9, 1974, p. 49.

Table 7

ESTIMATED PRIVATE SECTOR CAPITAL INVESTMENTS
FOR POLLUTION CONTROL, 1972–81
(billions of 1972 dollars)

Category	Amount
Air pollution	39.9
Water pollution	68.0
Radiation	1.2
Solid waste	2.9
Total	112.0

Source: U.S. Council on Environmental Quality, *Environmental Quality,* fourth annual report, 1973, p. 93.

recently quoted as making the following cavalier statement: "The whole thrust of the new legislation is to push technology and not get bogged down in deciding whether costs justify water-quality needs in a particular area." [17]

Because so much already has been written on industrial pollution control, the following chapters of this study will focus on some of the newer areas of government requirements, such as product safety and job health.

---

[17] Burt Schorr, "U.S. Water-Cleanup Rules, Due Out Shortly, to Cost Industry Far More than Predicted," *Wall Street Journal,* October 3, 1973, p. 32.

3

HIGHER COSTS OF
AUTOMOBILES

If there is one thing worse than GM producing cars, it would be the U.S. government producing them.

Ralph Nader

Much attention has been given to the nuisance involved in driving automobiles with federally mandated safety and environment features, but the higher cost of producing these vehicles and hence the higher prices paid by American motorists have received comparatively little attention.

The nuisance or discomfort involved is described graphically, although unwittingly, in the following excerpt from the Seat Belt System Owner's Guide issued by a major automobile manufacturer:

1. Get in your car.

2. Fasten your lap/shoulder harness.

    A. If you have a front seat passenger, his seatbelts must be fastened also, or the car will not start.

    B. If you have a package, handbag, briefcase, etc., weighing 25 lbs. or more, and have space only in the front seat, place the object on the front seat, and then buckle the passenger-side belt.

    C. If you have a dog weighing 25 lbs. or more occupying the passenger seat, buckle the passenger-side belt before attempting to start car.

    D. If the passenger-side belt is already buckled when you add the package, dog, or passenger, unbuckle, then rebuckle the belt before attempting to start car.

3. Start your car.
   A. If your car won't start, try unbuckling and rebuckling your belt (and your passenger's) to be sure the buckle was fully fastened.
   B. If that fails, turn the ignition key to "ON," then get out of your car and raise the hood. Press the bypass switch mounted on the fire wall to "START." Close the hood, get back in your car, buckle up, and turn your ignition all the way as in normal starting.
   C. If your car stalls, do not turn the ignition to "OFF" position. That way you can keep trying to start your car as often as necessary without leaving the car.
   D. If you accidentally turn the ignition key to "OFF," turn it back to "ON," unbuckle, get out of the car, open the hood, press the bypass switch again for another "free" start. (Incidentally, if the bypass switch is taped down, the action will be detected in the switch and cancelled.)
4. Drive the car.
   A. If your dog is on the floor when you begin driving the car, and then jumps on the seat and the passenger-side belt is unbuckled, a buzzer will sound. Stop the car and buckle the belt.
   B. In a somewhat rare situation, when driving over a very rough road, you may be bounced about in your seat. Should your engine be stopped, remain buckled in your seat and restart your car. A "bounce-time" delay (designed primarily to allow you to straighten your clothing after buckling up) also allows a restart in this situation.[1]

In a more colorful way, journalist Vic Gold described the scene at the National Safety Belt Conference, sponsored by Ralph Nader:

> Three grown men scrambling around, across, and over the front seat of one of those dangerous 1974 model horseless carriages, futilely wrestling with a network of elusive buckles and straps. . . . But if I am any judge of my fellow American non-stooges, Big Motherism in the safety-belt field has now gone too far.[2]

Judging by recent congressional legislation eliminating the interlock requirement, Gold's 1973 statement was prescient.

---

[1] Cited in Allstate Insurance advertisement in *Time*, April 15, 1974.

[2] Quoted in Carl H. Madden, *What's Wrong With Consumerism*, remarks at the Washington Journalism Center, Washington, D. C., December 10, 1973, p. 8.

The Cost to the Consumer

As would be expected, the ever more complicated safety system—as well as federally mandated pollution controls—are increasing the price of motor vehicles. Table 8 shows, *for the typical new* 1974 passenger automobile, the estimated cost of the successive changes required in the 1968–74 period to meet federal standards. According to these data, the federally mandated costs average $320 per car.[3] With new car purchases totalling about 9 million for 1974, American motorists thus paid approximately $3 billion extra for the governmentally imposed requirements.

In addition, the added weight and complexity of the mandated features have increased the operating costs of the vehicles, particularly the fuel costs. The cost of the new catalytic converters that will be required on 1975 automobiles is estimated at over $150 per vehicle.

The $3 billion that American new car buyers paid out in 1974 for the added features mandated by the federal government had a high "opportunity cost." We as a nation had to forego the opportunity to spend that very considerable sum on other ways of reducing road accidents. Just think what a fraction of the $1 billion that is being devoted to the "interlock" system alone could have yielded if applied to these alternatives:

(1) Identifying and eliminating the serious hazards created by unclear or badly located road signs, and placing signs where they are needed but are now absent.

(2) Providing more universal and more intensive driver instruction and testing, including the development of simulators that could be used to make driver training and testing more demanding, perhaps with no increase in cost.

(3) Assessing the cost and benefits of more thorough vehicle inspections, including the feasibility of combining safety inspections with checkups on pollution-control equipment and engine operation. This would help to meet safety, environment and energy conservation objectives simultaneously.[4]

Every benefit to the customer or the public may have a corresponding cost to the car buyer, who ultimately must pay for product

---

[3] These costs are underestimated because they utilize BLS data for each year and ignore the inflation that has occurred since. The BLS indices treat these added costs as measures of quality improvement.

[4] "The Bureaucrats Belt Us Again," *Fortune*, October 1973, p. 128.

Table 8

INCREASES IN PASSENGER AUTOMOBILE PRICES RESULTING FROM FEDERAL REQUIREMENTS, 1968–74
(estimated retail cost at time of introduction)

Model Year	Action	Price Per Car
1968	Seat and shoulder belt installations	$ 11.51
	HEW standards for exhaust emission systems	16.00
1968–69	Windshield defrosting and defogging systems	.70
	Windshield wiping and washing systems	1.25
	Door latches and hinge systems	.55
	Lamps, reflective devices and associated equipment	6.30
1969	Head restraints	16.65
1970	Lamps, reflective devices, and associated equipment	4.00
	HEW standards for exhaust emission systems	5.50
1968–70	Theft protection (steering, transmission, and ignition locking and buzzing system)	7.85
	Occupant protection in interior impact (glove box door remain closed on impact)	.35
1971	Fuel evaporative systems	19.00
1972	Improved exhaust emissions standards required by Clean Air Act	6.00
	Warranty changes resulting from federal requirement that all exhaust emission systems be warranted for 5 years or 50,000 miles	1.00
	Voluntarily added safety features in anticipation of future safety requirements	2.00
	Seat belt warning system and locking device on retractors	20.25
1972–73	Exterior protection (standard #215)	69.90
1973	Location, identification, and illumination of controls improvements	.60
	Reduced flammability of interior materials	5.80
1969–73	Improved side door strength	15.30
1974	Interlock system and other changes to meet federal safety requirements	107.60
	Improved exhaust emissions systems to comply with the Federal Clean Air Act	1.40
	Total	$319.51

Source: Computed from data supplied by the U.S. Department of Labor, Bureau of Labor Statistics.

changes. In the case of tougher bumpers, for example, any saving in insurance premiums or reduced car repair costs should be weighed against the additional cost of the bumper and the additional gasoline needed to move the cars made heavier by the new bumpers, supporting frame, and related equipment.

The present phase of governmental regulation of industry, particularly in the safety area, seems to be insensitive to the notion of seeking out the least costly way of achieving objectives. Professor Roger L. Miller of the University of Washington has described the problem as follows:

> Now they seem to be insisting that Detroit should begin producing what amounts to overly expensive tanks without giving much thought to some alternatives that are just as effective, while less costly to society.
>
> Modification or removal of roadside hazards might eliminate as many as one quarter of all motor vehicle fatalities. Another 10 percent or so occur when automobiles collide with bridge abutments, or with pier supports or overpasses.[5]

According to Professor Miller, most of these hazards could be eliminated by better marking of poorly marked roads and intersections, the installation of breakaway traffic signs and light poles, and the padding of abutments and concrete pillars. The benefit would go to owners and passengers of old cars, not just to those driving newer models with the required safety features. Moreover, 60 percent of drivers in fatal, single car crashes are drunk, as are 50 percent of the drivers at fault in fatal crashes involving two or more cars. This leads Miller to ask the obvious question: "Why should the many who purchase autos end up paying for increased safety in order to prevent fatalities involving the drunken drivers?"[6] A far less expensive alternative might be more vigorous legal prosecution of drunken drivers and drunken pedestrians. James B. Gregory, the head of the U.S. National Highway Safety Administration, has provided the following vivid description of the law enforcement problem:

> You find a man who is not dead drunk but certainly is not driving in a responsible manner. He is abusive to the enforcement officer . . . they finally get him in the back of the patrol car. He gets sick all over the back seat.

---

[5] Roger LeRoy Miller, *The Nader Files: An Economic Critique,* a paper presented at a Conference on Government and the Consumer at the Center for Government Policy and Business, October 22-28, 1973, p. 3.

[6] Ibid., p. 6.

They take him to the police station and he is immediately turned loose on his own recognizance, perhaps even to drive home.

He comes up before a justice, and he is let off or not constricted at all.[7]

Gregory states that many judges are reluctant to take harsh measures against a motorist who pleads that he has to drive to work to support his family. Professor Miller contends that decreasing the number of drunks driving or walking would seem to be more efficient than requiring every motorist to invest in expensive safety equipment. He also notes that few of the safety devices on automobiles are designed to protect pedestrians. The National Safety Council estimated that 38 percent of the people who died from motor vehicle accidents in 1971—21,000 out of 54,700—were pedestrians, bicyclists, motorcyclists, and others who could not have been helped by seat restraints of any kind.

Thus, when considering a proposal for new and costly governmental safety requirements the pertinent policy question is not the emotional one, "Are you more concerned with dollars than saving human lives?" It is, rather, the more cogent one, "What is the most effective way of achieving our safety objectives?"

On-the-Job Training Costs for Regulators

The recent upsurge in the number, variety, and extent of government programs to regulate business has revealed numerous deficiencies in the very process of regulation. Any reader of the "horror" stories that abound in the national press may, with good reason, jump to the conclusion that the regulators are undergoing some form of rudimentary on-the-job training, at the consumer's expense.

For example, a recent issue of the *New York Times* reported: "U.S. to Study Effects of Antipollution Devices." [8] What was revealing—and distressing—was to learn that this study was taking place *after* the U.S. Environmental Protection Agency had ordered automobile manufacturers to incorporate a specific and expensive antipollution device—the catalytic converter. Apparently, both private and governmental researchers have shown that the new "anti-pollution" equipment may produce harmful amounts of sulphuric acid mists, which

---

[7] Edward W. O'Brien, "State's Treatment of Drunk Drivers Called Lax," *St. Louis Globe-Democrat*, June 1, 1974, p. 11A.

[8] Edmund K. Gravely, Jr., "U.S. to Study Effects of Antipollution Devices," *New York Times*, April 7, 1974, Section 1A, p. 21.

can irritate the lungs. Also the catalytic converters emit platinum which, in the words of John B. Moran, the director of the EPA's fuel and additive research program, is "really adding a new thing to our environment." [9] It appears that there is no significant amount of platinum in our air or water at the present time. Just think of the governmental and public outrage that would have resulted if a private organization had taken such action without submitting a detailed environmental impact statement and without subjecting itself to the criticism of the various groups desiring to participate in the review process.

The $6 million that EPA is belatedly devoting to studying the adverse environmental effects of its actions is but the tip of the iceberg. Mr. Moran estimates that it would take several billion dollars for the oil companies to remove sulphur from gasoline. Moreover, desulphurization might adversely affect the supply of gasoline. A nearby article in the same issue of the *New York Times* reports numerous failures in the "interlock" system which another federal agency, the Federal Motor Vehicle Safety Commission, has required automotive manufacturers to put on all 1974 cars. A colorful but perhaps typical complaint about this system was reported in San Diego: "It's a devilish contraption to get into, and I've had to call a service truck three times to get the car started." [10]

The *New York Times* reported that a check of new car owners around the country shows that the government-mandated safety interlock system is "almost universally disliked," that many owners have had it disconnected, and that malfunctions sometimes keep cars from starting. The owner of a small car rental company in Miami stated that he disconnected all the interlocks on his first 1974 cars because his clients complained and because several cars broke down while in use. An automobile dealer described servicing trouble with the gadget as "fairly frequent." [11] These private costs resulting from government regulation, unfortunately, are not separately identified in any available statistics on the economy.

A sense of futility—a costly sense of futility—arises when we note that a recent study by the Institute for Highway Safety reports that 41 percent of the drivers of 1974 model automobiles have found ways to bypass the interlock system and avoid using seat belts.[12]

---

[9] Ibid., p. 21.

[10] "The Interlock System: A 'Devilish Contraption,'" *New York Times*, April 7, 1974, Section 1A, p. 20.

[11] Ibid.

[12] "41 Pct. Bypass Buzzers," *St. Louis Post-Dispatch*, August 2, 1974, p. 2A.

4

HIGHER COSTS OF CONSUMER PRODUCTS

When it involves a product that is unsafe, I don't care how much it costs the company to correct the problem.

> R. David Pittle, member, Consumer Product Safety Commission

"You've got so much power here it's unbelievable. . . . You've got life or death over whether consumers have anything to consume," said Congressman Jamie Whitten, chairman of a House appropriations subcommittee on consumer protection to the chairman of the relatively new Consumer Product Safety Commission (CPSC).[1]

This commission is an important although often overlooked addition to the already impressive array of governmental agencies that regulate one or more facets of business decision making. It has jurisdiction over more than 10,000 products and possesses the authority to set mandatory safety standards, to ban or recall products from the marketplace without a court hearing, to require warnings by manufacturers, to order rebates to consumers, and even to send offending executives to jail.[2]

The likelihood of the CPSC's using the full extent of its power may be remote. Yet, the judicious, restrained approach that might have been expected from the wielders of such awesome power is not apparent in the public statements of the commission members. As commission chairman, Richard O. Simpson blithely puts it, "You name it and CPSC probably has jurisdiction over it."[3] That this statement

---

[1] William H. Miller, "Consumer Product Safety Commission: What You Don't Know Can Hurt You," *Industry Week*, October 29, 1973, p. 38.

[2] Consumer Product Safety Act, Public Law 92-573.

[3] Robert T. Gray, "Washington's New Little Giant," *Nation's Business*, September 1973, p. 21.

is not merely rhetoric can be seen in the commission's current plans to declare the average residence an unsafe product and thus bring the entire home into the agency's jurisdiction. Chairman Simpson's attitude on enforcement does little to foster better business-government relations: "If a company violates our statute, we will not concern ourselves with its middle-level executives; we will put the chief executive in jail. Once we do put a top executive behind bars, I am sure that we will get a much higher degree of compliance from other companies." [4]

Another CPSC commissioner, R. David Pittle, provides a more graphic analogy to violence: "Any time consumer safety is threatened, we're going to go for the company's throat." [5] There seems little awareness on the part of the commission's members of the difficulties involved in developing new regulatory approaches, of the degrees and range of product safety, or even of the possibility that they may make mistakes. To quote Mr. Pittle again, "When it involves a product that is unsafe, I don't care how much it costs the company to correct the problem." [6]

The Impact on Consumers

Unless the Consumer Product Safety Commission reverses its course, its actions are likely to produce major increases in the prices that consumers pay for the products they use—and only questionable benefits. Although the commission seems oblivious to it, it is consumers who ultimately pay for the changes that are required. The first suit filed in St. Louis by the Consumer Product Safety Commission in January 1974 may indicate the extent of the "overkill" in the commission's approach to safeguarding consumers from potential hazards. The offending items were 1,494 containers of windshield washer solvent which were without child-proof caps and were not labeled with the required statement, "Cannot be made nonpoisonous." [7] What remedy did the commission seek? That the caps be changed and the necessary four words of bureaucratese be posted on each of the bottles? Hardly. Instead, it ordered that each and

---

[4] Gerald R. Rosen, " 'We're Going for Companies' Throats,' " Dun's Review, January 1973, p. 36.

[5] Ibid.

[6] Ibid., p. 38.

[7] "Hardware Store Is Sued Over Hazardous Solvent," St. Louis Post-Dispatch, January 3, 1974. Follow-up interview on July 23, 1974, with officials of the Ace Hardware Company in St. Louis, Missouri.

every one of the 1,494 containers of windshield washing material be destroyed—thereby no doubt contributing to the nation's pollution problem. And those of us who use that kind of solvent in our cars (and drink more conventional fluids) of course wind up paying the higher price that results from this federally mandated waste.

But this is only part of the story. The company involved, Ace Hardware, did not contest the CPSC ruling, and offered to destroy the material or turn it over to a CPSC representative. It was discovered, however, that no CPSC official was authorized to accept the contraband and that the company was prohibited from destroying it. Months later, after a court order was obtained, a duly authorized officer of the law appeared at the company to confiscate the goods.

In another interesting case, the commission ordered formal hearings to determine if 4 million electric frying pans were hazardous. One fascinating aspect of this case is that, out of the 4 million pans, not a single injury had been reported by the commission![8] It is no exaggeration to suggest that the commission—unwittingly of course— may turn out to be the most anti-consumer organization of all time. This paradoxical result would be brought about by the commission's forcing such expensive complexity on the manufacturers of consumer products that poor, and even middle-income, families would be priced out of the market.

Professor Max Brunk of Cornell University gets to the heart of the matter: Consumerism is intended to protect the consumer; but look what the regulations do to the consumer "who pays the cost and loses the benefits that a prohibited product or service could have provided."[9] Not much reflection is required to see that business can adjust to these controls more easily than can the consumer, because it can pass on the added costs that result.

Professor Brunk notes that consumerists sometimes have as much difficulty in convincing the consumer of his or her need for protection as they do in convincing a regulatory body to provide the protection.[10] Experience under the truth-in-lending law furnishes a good example. Has the compulsory requirement to show true interest costs slowed down the growth of consumer debt or the rise in interest rates? On the contrary, since the passage of the act, the ratio of consumer debt to consumer income has reached an all-time high and interest rates,

---

[8] "Some Fry Pans and Chain Saws May Be Unsafe," *St. Louis Post-Dispatch*, January 15, 1974, p. 8A.

[9] Max E. Brunk, "Consumerism and Marketing," in *Issues in Business and Society*, ed. George Steiner (New York: Random House, 1972), p. 462.

[10] Ibid., p. 463.

for many reasons, have risen sharply. The average credit purchaser still is more interested in the full amount of the monthly payment than in the amount (and rate) of interest included in it. Similarly, despite the justification for unit pricing as a means of helping low-income families to stretch their food dollar by buying more intelligently, available surveys show that it is the high-income, well-educated customers who are most aware of this information.[11]

In the area of product safety, it should be recognized that consumers have unequal tastes for safety, as well as for other characteristics of product performance. Policy makers should realize, particularly where the safety hazard is minor (the occasional blister on a finger), that very large cost increases may deprive many consumers of the use of many products, which would hardly be a contribution to human welfare. In the words of Professor J. Fred Weston of UCLA, there is a need to recognize trade-offs between safety and other criteria important to consumers.[12]

For example, a power tool selling for $20 may not have the capability of being in use for more than an hour, while the $500 tool may safely be used for a much longer period. Even though the instructions on the tools are very clear in this respect, some consumers may willingly buy the cheaper model and knowingly take the chance of burning it out. A policy of complete product safety would ban the cheaper model, thereby effectively depriving the low-income consumer of buying a power tool at all. Similarly, we could decrease the risk of injury from kitchen knives by making them less sharp, but that would reduce their ease of operation and usefulness. As Steven Kelman phrases it, "The question is always whether the safety improvement is worth its cost in money or convenience."[13]

The Impact on Business

The record-keeping burden implied by some of the Consumer Product Safety Commission's early actions is substantial. In its first major proposed rule in August 1973, the commission called on every manufacturer, distributor, or retailer—upon learning that a product it sold "creates a substantial risk of injury"—to provide the commission with a staggering array of information, including: the number of products

---

[11] Ibid., p. 465.

[12] J. Fred Weston, "Economic Aspects of Consumer Product Safety," in *Issues in Business and Society*, p. 499.

[13] Steven Kelman, "Regulation By the Numbers—A Report on the Consumer Product Safety Commission," *Public Interest*, Summer 1974, p. 86.

which present a hazard or potential hazard; the number of units of each product involved; the number of units of each product in the hands of consumers; specific dates when the faulty units were manufactured and distributed; an accounting of when and where such products (and the number of units of each) were distributed; the model and serial numbers affected; a list of names and addresses of every distributor, retailer, and producer, if known; a description of the effort that has been made to notify consumers of the defect; and, details of corrective tests, quality controls, and engineering changes made or contemplated.[14] The "reporting" requirement is not fulfilled until the company submits a final report indicating that the "potential" product hazard has been corrected. Thus, the commission shifts to the company the full burden of determining and remedying potential product defects—and in the background there is the ever-present threat of criminal sanctions should the commission disagree with the company's decisions.

In fairness to the commission, it should be noted that it has turned down the most outrageous demands of the professional "consumer advocates." For example, it rejected the petition of Ralph Nader's Health Research Group, which warned of the "imminent hazard to the public health" represented by lead-wick candles. The petition asserted that small children might chew or swallow the candles, taking lead into their systems and candle-lit suppers would result in "meals literally bathed in lead." In a letter to the Nader group, Commissioner Laurence M. Kushner stated that the petition "was drawn either with abysmal ignorance of elementary physical science, colossal intent to deceive the public or both. The calculations, in the petition, of possible concentrations of lead in air which might result from burning such candles were based on assumptions that are physically impossible. . . ." [15]

The Power of Government Regulation

In the words of Arnold Elkind, chairman of the National Commission on Product Safety whose recommendations led to the creation of the CPSC: "It's true that the CPSC may be the most powerful independent regulatory agency ever created. . . . But it has to be. It has to have a wide choice of weapons to cope with the diverse range of situations it confronts." [16]

---

[14] *Federal Register*, vol. 38, no. 149 (August 3, 1973).

[15] "Please Don't Eat the Candles," *Wall Street Journal*, January 16, 1974, p. 12.

[16] Miller, "Consumer Product Safety Commission," p. 41.

Of all the federal regulatory agencies, the commission provides the most obvious example of the excesses of Big Motherism. Not content with ordering companies to follow specific practices, it has taken to providing gratuitous advice to the public. One of its press releases, "CPSC Issues Safety Tips on Winter Sports," contains the following gems:

> A number of accidents happened when the skier was tired. . . . Take lessons from an expert. Studies show that beginners are hurt more frequently, so advancement is desirable. . . .
> Skiers should use good quality equipment that fits well. . . . Skaters should never skate close to open bodies of water.[17]

And in its "Special Holiday Issue" dated October 1, 1973, the commission offers the following advice for parents:

> Choose all toys carefully. . . . Choose carefully and selectively.
> Choose a toy appropriate for the child's age and development.
> Avoid toys that produce excessive noise.
> Check instructions.
> Supervise young children at play.
> Don't leave indoor toys outdoors overnight.
> Moisture may cause damage.
> Remember, rusting leads to structural weakening of components.
> Toys should be put away on shelves or in a toy box where they cannot be broken or cause someone to trip.[18]

The Consumer Product Safety Commission apparently also is infected with the virus of empire-building. One commissioner has reportedly argued that a house is "a hazardous consumer product" and thus qualifies for CPSC regulation.[19] Enforcement would be difficult. To achieve compliance, it was suggested that local building codes incorporate the commission's regulations so that local inspectors would be required to enforce the commission's standards!

---

[17] U.S. Consumer Product Safety Commission, *Safety Tips on Winter Sports*, Press Release, December 16, 1973, p. 1.

[18] U.S. Consumer Product Safety Commission, *Banned Products*, vol. 2, part 1 (October 1, 1973), section titled "Give Your Children Playtime Fun with Safety."

[19] "CPSC May Set Housing Standards," *Industry Week*, January 7, 1974, p. 61.

Perhaps it is the commission's September 1973 press release on back-to-school hazards that set a new high for Big Motherism. James J. Kilpatrick quoted it in part: "Sharpened pencils, shiny scissors, new paints and brightly colored metal lunchboxes with matching vacuum bottles may bring delight and pride on the first day of school, but they can also bring howls of pain and even serious injury if they are not selected and used with care." Mr. Kilpatrick commented: "Is that not splendid? We have needed a Federal agency to tell us these things."[20]

Although these press releases may represent a relatively harmless waste of the taxpayers' money, other actions by the commission could have more serious consequences for the economy and the society. For example, the CPSC appears to have taken the position, perhaps unwittingly, that a product manufacturer is guilty until proved innocent. This surprising position seems implicit in the following CPSC decree reported on October 1, 1973: "Articles not meeting the requirements of the regulation are to be considered as banned even though they have not yet been reviewed, confirmed as banned, and added to the Banned Products List by the Consumer Product Safety Commission."[21]

Moreover, in its zeal for its task, the Consumer Product Safety Commission seems to be moving to new levels of high-handedness. Although the commission is charged with the responsibility for product safety, its members are trying to pass on part of this responsibility to newspapers and magazines. In a recent session with reporters, commission members stated their belief that publishers should attempt to verify the safety of the products advertised in their publications. CPSC chairman Simpson was quoted as saying that newspapers and magazines that carry advertisements should consider hiring specialists to inspect the products involved or should farm out the task to outside consultants.[22] Thus, producers and distributors would have to satisfy not only the federally chartered Consumer Product Safety Commission but also the private safety inspectors appointed by each individual private publication!

The stepped-up pace of CPSC regulation is resulting in "reverse distribution"—that is, product recalls—becoming an important part of the marketing cost of many companies. In addition to automobile

---

[20] James J. Kilpatrick, "New Federal Agency's 'Frankenstein' Look," *St. Louis Globe-Democrat*, October 24, 1973, p. 16.

[21] U.S. Consumer Product Safety Commission, *Banned Products*, October 1, 1973, p. 1.

[22] "Consumer Agency Is Critical of Ads," *New York Times*, February 13, 1974, p. 47.

companies, increasing numbers of manufacturers of TV sets, bicycles, ovens, and other nonautomotive products are being involved in recall situations. This relatively new activity requires a major record-keeping effort so that owners of a recalled product can be promptly notified. Also, an expanded network of service firms is necessary to replace the substandard parts or substitute new products.

The Consumer Product Safety Commission has indicated that it ultimately may require manufacturers to keep records of all product complaints and to make them available to the commission if it so requests. This information could form the basis for additional product recalls. It is likely that more consumer complaint letters will be kept in company files—and perhaps acted on.

The cost of recalls varies with the number of products sold, the amount of time and effort required to track down the purchasers, and the percentage of products that require repair, replacement, or refund. It cost General Motors $3.5 million for postage alone to notify by certified mail, as required by law, the 6.5 million owners of cars with questionable engine mounts. Some companies even have conducted "dry runs" of recall procedures.

Labels and Labeling

The CPSC, of course, is not the only consumer guardian that the Congress has established. More traditional programs, ranging from controlling the production and distribution of drugs to regulating the sale of pet turtles, are located in the Department of Agriculture and the Department of Health, Education, and Welfare.

One typical government response to rising consumerist pressures now takes the form of stricter controls over product labeling, that is, requirements that package labels set forth specific information on contents and usage. One court recently held that the standard of clarity applicable to a package label is not what the label says to "the reasonable consumer," but rather what it communicates to "the ignorant, the unthinking and credulous. . . ." [23]

"What's in a name?"—asks the U.S. Department of Agriculture. It answers its own question: "Plenty, when a meat or poultry product bears the mark of federal inspection!" [24] It turns out that the term "plenty" is no overstatement. The instructions to the producers of beef products are quite intriguing. Products labeled "beef with

---

[23] Cited in "Social Issues Briefs," *Business Week*, May 18, 1974, p. 78.

[24] U.S. Department of Agriculture, Animal and Plant Health Inspection Service, *Standards for Meat and Poultry Products*, 1973, p. 1.

Table 9
FEDERAL STANDARDS FOR POULTRY

Item	Minimum Percentage of Poultry Meat Required
Poultry almondine	50
Poultry barbecue	40
Poultry paella	35[a]
Poultry hash	30
Poultry chili	28
Poultry croquettes	25
Poultry cacciatore	20[b]
Poultry casserole	18
Poultry chili with beans	17
Poultry tetrazzini	15
Poultry pies	14
Poultry brunswick stew	12[c]
Cabbage stuffed with poultry	8
Cannelloni with poultry	7
Poultry tamales	6
Poultry chop suey	4
Chop suey with poultry	2

[a] Or 35 percent poultry meat and other meat (cooked basis); no more than 35 percent cooked rice; must contain seafood.

[b] Or 40 percent with bone.

[c] Must contain corn.

Source: Computed from U.S. Department of Agriculture, Animal and Plant Health Inspection Service, *Standards for Meat and Poultry Products*, 1973, pp. 6-7.

gravy," for example, must contain at least 50 percent cooked beef, whereas those labeled "gravy with beef" require only 35 percent cooked beef. "Beef and dumplings with gravy" must have only 25 percent beef, as must "beef and gravy with dumplings." But "beef and pasta in tomato sauce" can get by with as little as 17.5 percent beef.[25]

At times the Department of Agriculture standard setters demonstrate a certain elegance: "Beef Burgundy," in addition to being at least 50 percent beef, must contain enough wine "to characterize the sauce." [26] Meeting the requirements for poultry dishes, in contrast, is an exercise in straightforward arithmetic. The permutations and combinations are so numerous that they can best be presented in tabular form (see Table 9). The manufacture of poultry products

[25] Ibid., p. 1.
[26] Ibid., p. 2.

Figure 1

FEDERAL CONSUMER PROTECTION LAWS,
1890–1972

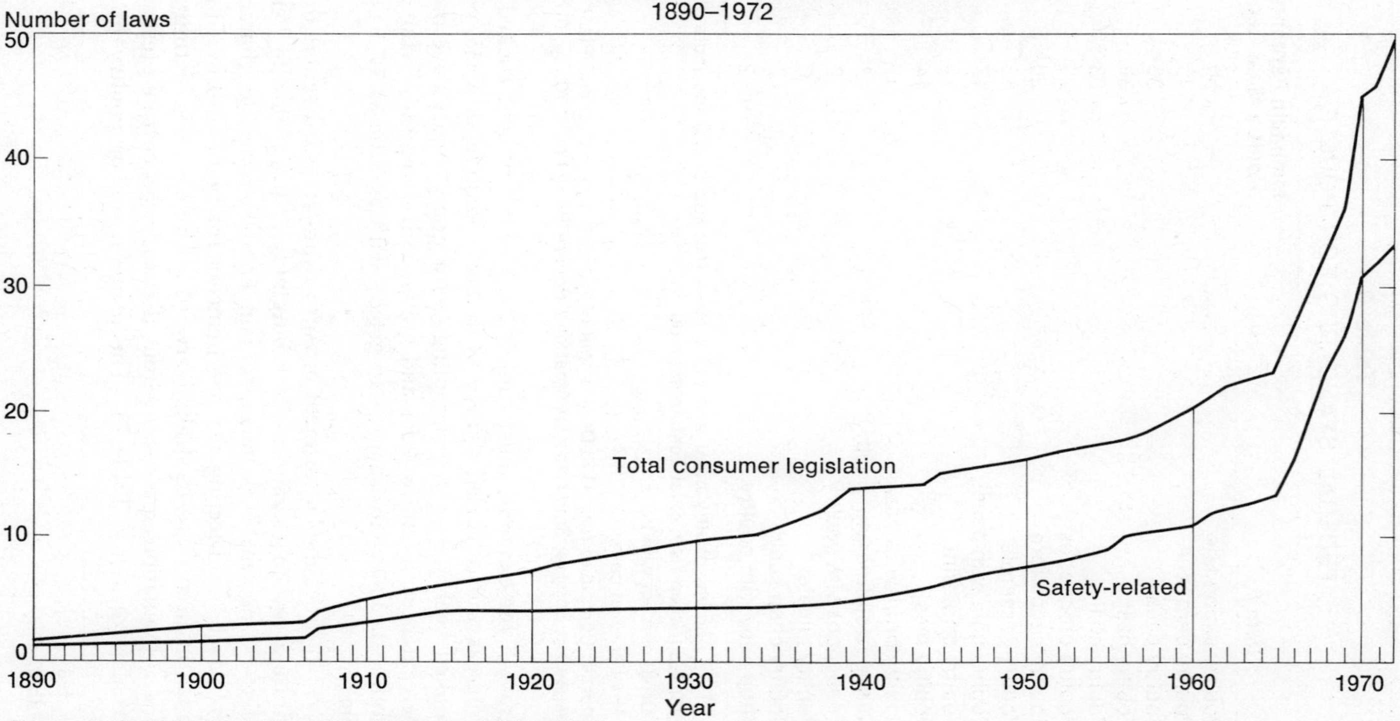

Source: National Business Council for Consumer Affairs, 1973.

literally is becoming an exercise in "doing it by the numbers," with the numbers selected by a federal agency.

Outlook

The recent upsurge in federal legislation related to consumer interests is depicted in Figure 1. Although an upward trend has been visible since the turn of the century, a rapid acceleration in the frequency of new control legislation began in the mid-1960s and shows little sign of diminishing. Not only have more laws been passed since then, but also the laws are broader and more far-reaching.

5

HIGHER COSTS OF INDUSTRIAL PRODUCTION

> . . . the Main Street merchant who recently attended an Occupational Safety and Health Act seminar was asked the next day if he had profited from the meeting. He replied "Oh, yes, I've already bought the sign required by OSHA. . . . The one that is so high and so wide and says, 'For Sale.' "
>
> Senate Committee on Small Business

The Occupational Safety and Health Act is one of those regulatory innovations whose objectives are so worthy that critics questioning the actual conduct of the effort are put on the defensive to prove that they are not devoid of human compassion. After all, who is not in favor of improving a work environment in which over 14,000 Americans were killed in 1973 in job-related accidents? But, on the other hand, by what stretch of the imagination does an OSHA rule calling for daily cleaning of spittoons help to reduce the number of casualties?

Even so sympathetic an organization as the Federation of American Scientists has chided the administration of OSHA. It made the following criticism in a statement issued in 1973:

> Regulations are voluminous and complex; the language is convoluted beyond recognition except by a scientist or lawyer. Worse yet, there is no provision for a penalty-free consultation with an Occupational Safety and Health Administration inspector. . . .
>
> The Occupational Safety and Health Act, in short, has surfaced at least as many problems as it was designed to solve.[1]

---

[1] "Statement of the Council of the Federation of American Scientists," *FAS Newsletter*, June 1973, p. 1.

OSHA's regulations are so lengthy and tedious that the agency's own representatives are not always aware of them all. For example, when my research assistant checked the reference to spittoons, he was assured by the area representative (and in fairly colorful language) that no such provision existed. That assurance notwithstanding, the OSHA regulations as published in the *Federal Register* contain the following statement: "Cuspidors are considered undesirable, but, if used, they shall be of such construction that they are cleanable. They shall be cleaned at least daily when in use (Title 29, Section 1910, 141 (a) (z) (ii))."

The most severe criticism of the Occupational Safety and Health Administration has come not from businessmen or labor but from within the federal government itself, namely, from Chairman Robert D. Moran of the Occupational Safety and Health Review Commission, the independent agency created to hear appeals from rulings by OSHA inspectors: "far too many standards are, to paraphrase Winston Churchill, 'riddles wrapped in mysteries inside enigmas.' They don't give the employer even a nebulous suggestion of what he should do to protect his employees from whatever-it-is, also left unexplained, which represents a hazard to their safety and health." [2] After citing one vague and general standard, Moran lamented: "What do you think it tells us to do? I have no idea—and I don't think OSHA could tell you, either, before an inspection, citation, complaint, hearing and post-hearing brief." [3] Moran concluded: "I submit that there isn't a person on earth who can be certain he is in full compliance with the requirements of this standard at any particular point of time." [4]

A major problem arises when the small employer needs help in interpreting the standards promulgated by a federal regulatory agency such as OSHA. He normally cannot afford to employ a staff of experts, so he logically looks to the government for guidance about his obligations. In the case of OSHA, he is given a singularly unhelpful pamphlet which devotes twenty-four pages of fine print merely to list the applicable standards for "general industry." The descriptive material is quite sparse. In fact, the section on "How to Use This Guide" is quoted below in its entirety!

---

[2] Robert D. Moran, "Our Job Safety Law Should Say What It Means," *Nation's Business*, April 1974, p. 23.

[3] Ibid., p. 25.

[4] Ibid.

To be used effectively, this Guide must be considered as a:

1. companion piece to the master document, 29 CFR 1910, Occupational Safety and Health Standards for General Industry.

2. key index to all the standards in 29 CFR 1910, which have been classified under the six categories, and the administrative regulations drawn from Parts 1903, 1904, 1905, 1911, and 1912.

To find the desired information the user should first read the introductory statement to each category. Then, he should analyze the hazard and classify it according to the workplace, machines and equipment, materials, the employee, a special process, or a power source. By looking up the applicable category, the location of the applicable standard in 29 CFR can be found. Since hazards may be logically classified in more than one category, look under each category which might apply to your situation.[5]

It is hardly surprising that William S. Lowe, chairman of the board of A. P. Green Refractories Company, told a House subcommittee on environmental problems that OSHA "is presently creating more concern within the small business community than any other legislation passed in recent years."[6]

Ladders, Exits, and Other Trivia

Nevertheless, let us attempt to follow the procedure described in the OSHA guide cited above. As the guide instructs, the standards themselves are in something called "29 CFR 1910." Let us assume that somehow we know that this is legalese for the Code of Federal Regulations and that we are to turn to Title 29, which deals with labor, and that we ultimately get to Part 1910, which deals with occupational safety and health standards.

But brace yourself. Document 29 CFR 1910 contains 455 pages of fine print, including algebraic and trigonometric equations. Let us skip over the obviously technical parts and turn to the section dealing with something supposedly simple—ladders. To begin with, we are offered a definition: "a ladder is an appliance usually consisting of two side rails joined at regular intervals by crosspieces called steps,

---

[5] U.S. Occupational Safety and Health Administration, *Guide for Applying Safety and Health Standards, 29 CFR 1910, General Industry*, 1972, p. 1.

[6] Statement by William S. Lowe before the Subcommittee on Environmental Problems Affecting Small Business of the House Select Committee on Small Business, 92d Congress, 2d session (June 21, 1972), p. 1.

rungs, or cleats, on which a person may step in ascending or descending." [7] However, that just initiates our education into the subject. We next have to identify the various types of ladders. Our old friend the stepladder is, we are informed, "a self-supporting portable ladder, nonadjustable in length, having flat steps and a hinged back. Its size is designated by the overall length of the ladder measured along the front edge of the side rail." We are then led through similar detail on the single ladder, the extension ladder, the sectional ladder, the trestle ladder, the extension trestle ladder, the special-purpose ladder, the trolley ladder, and the side-rolling ladder. Thereupon, perhaps still amused that a tax-supported official has had the time and inclination for this type of activity, we find a bloated but unhelpful definition of "wood characteristics." The reader is informed that "wood characteristics are distinguishing features which by their extent and number determine the quality of a piece of wood." [8]

By now, the reader's eye may begin to wander. But OSHA's authors seem to have anticipated that, for in the very next column of fine print they have produced once again a definition of ladder— word for word the same definition from the previous page and followed by identical definitions of step ladder and all the other types of ladders previously enumerated, including the trolley ladder and the side-rolling ladder. Thereafter, in the very next column, comes yet another complete rendition of all of the definitions of the types of ladders.

The determined reader may push on to another section of the regulations of this supposedly simple subject. If he is lucky, he will pass over the following gem:

The angle (a) between the loaded and unloaded rails and the horizontal is to be calculated from the trigonometric equation:

$$\text{Sine a} = \frac{\text{Difference in deflection}}{\text{Ladder width}} \text{ [9]}$$

Let us assume that, on this first reading, our typical small businessman finds the subject of ladders just too complicated. Turning pages, he comes across an item that seems like it would be simpler —"Exit." For a starter, he learns that "Exit is that portion of a means of egress which is separated from all other spaces of the building or structure by construction or equipment as required in this subpart to

---

[7] *Federal Register*, vol. 37, no. 202 (October 18, 1972), p. 22105.

[8] Ibid., p. 22106.

[9] Ibid., p. 22118.

provide a protected way of travel to the exit discharge." [10] Our typical businessman, being a persevering fellow, realizes that this subject, too, is more complicated than he had thought. Clearly, he must learn about "means of egress" and "exit discharge." OSHA does not disappoint him:

> A means of egress is a continuous and unobstructed way of exit travel from any point in a building or structure to a public way and consists of three separate and distinct parts: the way of exit access, the exit, and the way of exit discharge. A means of egress comprises the vertical and horizontal ways of travel and shall include intervening room spaces, doorways, hallways, corridors, passageways, balconies, ramps, stairs, enclosures, lobbies, escalators, horizontal exits, courts, and yards.
>
> Exit discharge is that portion of a means of egress between the termination of an exit and a public way.[11]

At this point, our small businessman may be forgiven if he closes the OSHA guide and turns to his dictionary. There he finds solace: no mention of means of egress or exit discharges, and no definitions of exit which contain the word exit. Exit is simply "a passage or way out"! [12]

In the words of the Federation of American Scientists, "businessmen who have no legal or scientific training are unable to understand OSHA regulations. Unfortunately, few efforts are being made to translate this information into readable language. . . . Equally unnerving to the businesses is the sheer volume of the regulations—thousands of them apply to one small operation." [13]

The result of OSHA's activities—and of other new federal regulatory efforts as well—is to increase the overhead expenses of many manufacturers. In fact, a growth market has developed for organizations that provide services to companies that are trying to accommodate to ever more complex agency instructions.

Lack of a Sense of Proportion

In a recent interview, Chairman Moran of the Occupational Safety and Health Review Commission stated that many of OSHA's regula-

---

[10] Ibid., p. 22130.

[11] Ibid.

[12] *The American Heritage Dictionary of the English Language* (Boston: Houghton Mifflin Co., 1969).

[13] *FAS Newsletter*, June 1973, p. 4. See also Jack R. Nicholas, Jr., "OSHA, Big Government, and Small Business," *MSU Business Topics*, Winter 1973, p. 61.

tions are out of date. Further, according to Moran, the worst flaw is that many regulations are so lacking in uniformity that employers do not know how to comply and employees are not in a position to know when a regulation has been violated.[14]

Part of OSHA's problem apparently is not being able to distinguish between serious health hazards and mere trivia. Most citizens will support the agency's efforts to eliminate work environments which are associated with lethal hazards,[15] but will wonder, in exasperation or even alarm, why the agency wastes its time promulgating and rescinding a variety of standards concerning the specific dimensional requirements for partitions between toilets!

Take the case of the rubber gloves, one that the author pursued personally. After reading complaints from industry about unnecessary OSHA standards for electrical rubber gloves, the author requested detail from a knowledgeable Missouri engineer who had worked for half a century in the electrical field. The relevant parts of the engineer's reply follow:

> During all that period, I have never observed or heard of an accident due to failure of electrical rubber gloves *in service.* One must understand, I believe, the procedures, practices and daily use of these gloves to understand this record.
>
> First, each glove is electrically tested by the manufacturer before shipment. Upon receipt of these gloves they are again electrically tested by the utility or a testing laboratory and stamped with a number. Then each lineman is issued at least two pairs of gloves—and the numbers recorded. He uses one pair and before using it in his daily work he gives it an "air test" which is done by twirling the cuffs and forcing the entrapped air into the fingers. Obviously—if there is a hole—the air escapes. Meanwhile—his second pair is on test and he changes gloves once every week or two weeks.
>
> After usage—there are of course gloves that fail on test and are replaced. But it is the continual testing that I have described that prevents accidents while gloves are being used.
>
> I hope this information may be of interest to you. I am sure you are aware that a leather protector glove is worn over the rubber gloves when in use.[16]

[14] Pamela Meyer, "Even Its Own Chairman Frustrated, Confused By Controversial OSHA," *St. Louis Post-Dispatch,* March 1, 1974, p. 5C.

[15] See Paul Brodeur, "Annals of Industry: Casualties of the Workplace," *New Yorker,* November 19, 1973, pp. 87-149.

[16] Letter to the author dated June 17, 1974, from Clarence H. LeVee, retired vice president of engineering, A. B. Chance Company.

Perhaps more striking is the case of the government standards on mechanical presses. These standards distinguish between new and old installations, giving manufacturers additional time to make the expensive changes in brake and electrical systems required to bring their old installations into compliance. However, a supplementary directive states that if an employer moves a press more than "a short distance, for example, to provide additional aisle space," then the press qualifies as a new installation and therefore has to comply as if it were new. One result, in the words of a small industry executive, is that the small businessman is placed in a position where "he feels that moving his equipment around in his shop to accommodate production or expanded facilities must be done in a clandestine manner...." [17]

At times, it may be difficult to justify the record-keeping burden imposed on very small firms. Consider the case of the small printing shop with three employees. The statistics of the National Safety Council show that the disabling injury rate of the printing and publishing industry is 9.72 per 1 million man-hours of work. This means, assuming our small employer is average for his industry, that his three-man work force is likely to suffer one disabling injury every sixteen years.

Some OSHA rules clearly appear to be contradictory. For example, OSHA mandates backup alarms on vehicles at construction sites. Yet simultaneously it requires some employees to wear earplugs as a protection against noise, thus making it extremely difficult to hear the alarms.[18]

Perhaps even more serious than the inefficiency in the job safety and health program is the possibility of biased decision making. One example relates to the U.S. National Institute for Occupational Safety and Health (NIOSH), the agency that does the basic research underlying new OSHA regulations. Because of "budget limitations," NIOSH signed an agreement with the Amalgamated Clothing Workers under which an official federal study of safety and health hazards in the clothing industry is to be conducted by a union employee and financed by the union. The union agreed to pay the salary of an industrial hygienist, Dr. Peter J. Nord, to perform the study. In the words of the OSHA publication reporting the undertaking, "Although Nord will work full-time within NIOSH, he is an employee of the union rather than of the federal government. . . . The union will help

---

17 Statement by Lowe, p. 8.
18 "OSHA Under Attack," *Time*, July 8, 1974, p. 48.

obtain the cooperation of plant managers." [19] The agreement appears to be authorized by existing statute. Section 22(e)(6) of the Occupational Safety and Health Act provides that NIOSH may "accept and utilize the services of voluntary and noncompensated personnel." Perhaps the statute needs to be amended to require NIOSH to use common sense in applying it, although a mere administrative proclamation to guarantee impartiality should suffice.

Is the Objective to Punish or to Improve Conditions?

The implementation of the Occupational Safety and Health Act provides a pertinent example of how administrators can lose sight of their assigned objective. Because the act makes no provision for "courtesy inspections," a company cannot request an inspector to come to the plant without laying itself open to instant citations for some infraction of the OSHA rules and regulations. In order to "get around" this problem, one regional office of OSHA suggests that companies send photographs of their premises for off-site review by OSHA inspectors. After all, if the inspectors do not actually "see" the violation, they cannot issue a citation for it.[20]

The basic purpose of the Occupational Safety and Health Act is not to punish businessmen or to seek out the most costly method of meeting the statutory requirements, but rather to achieve a higher level of job safety. One would think that OSHA would welcome voluntary requests by business firms seeking to know whether their facilities meet safety standards. Because small firms usually lack the in-house safety departments maintained by larger companies, it is not surprising that it is the smaller companies that are frequently cited by OSHA inspectors for violations.

Without much public attention, the administration of the Occupational Safety and Health Act appears to have placed the responsibility for an individual's actions in safeguarding his or her own well-being entirely on the employer. In one case, the OSHA hearing officer held that merely providing earmuffs was not enough. "To avoid violation, the equipment also must be 'used,' and the final responsibility to assure that use rests with the employer." [21] The agency's

---

[19] "Unique Agreement Signed for Study of Clothing Industry," *Job Safety and Health,* March 1974, p. 31.

[20] "Get an OSHA 'Inspection' without Citation Risk," *Industry Week,* September 17, 1973, p. 9.

[21] James C. Hyatt, "Complex Issues Raised by Job Safety Act—Like Earmuff Dispute—Flood Commission," *Wall Street Journal,* January 30, 1973, p. 40.

regulations shift other responsibilities in a similar way: "Where employees provide their own protective equipment, the employer shall be responsible to assure its adequacy, including proper maintenance, and sanitation of such equipment." [22]

Cost of Government Controls

Estimates of current industry expenditures to meet government safety or other requirements are often no more than reasonable guesses. Survey results are not easy to interpret. It is often difficult for a company to separate clearly investment to meet federal requirements and investment in production equipment which would be purchased in the absence of the governmental restriction. Thus, the data in Table 10 should be taken mainly as illustrative of the substantial costs involved in meeting federally mandated requirements. In some cases, safety and health investment is reported to be a significant part of an industry's total capital spending. In 1972, 8 percent of the textile industry's investments and 12 percent of steel's were so related.[23]

According to the McGraw-Hill Department of Economics, already planned industrial investments in health and safety equipment are estimated to rise from $2.5 billion in 1972 to $3.4 billion in 1977. To some unspecified extent—that is, to the extent that these capital outlays succeed in reducing job-related injuries and illnesses—they can be considered as a form of investment in employee productivity.

A recent study commissioned by the Occupational Safety and Health Administration estimates that it will cost American industry an aggregate of $13.5 billion to bring existing facilities into compliance with the current OSHA noise standard of 90 A scale decibels (dBA). If the more stringent standard of 85 dBA is adopted—and this is the recommendation of the U.S. National Institute for Occupational Safety and Health—the compliance cost is expected to increase to $31.6 billion (see Table 11). Hearings on the NIOSH proposal have been scheduled. The more stringent standard is supported by the Environmental Protection Agency.[24]

In evaluating the merits of such an investment, an economist is concerned not only with the magnitude of the resources involved, but also with the alternative uses to which those resources could be

---

[22] *Federal Register*, October 18, 1972, p. 22230.

[23] "The High Price of Job Safety," *Business Week*, May 26, 1973, p. 27.

[24] "OSHA Noise Standard Compliance Could Cost Industry $13.5 Billion," *Washington Report*, February 11, 1974, p. 4; "The Expensive Sound of Silence," *Business Week*, July 20, 1974, p. 28.

Table 10

ESTIMATED COMPLIANCE COSTS OF
OSHA SAFETY STANDARDS, BY INDUSTRY

($ in millions)

Industry	Investment in Employee Safety and Health		
	1972	1973	Percent change
Manufacturing:			
Stone, clay, and glass	30	87	+190
Miscellaneous transportation equipment	6	15	+150
Rubber	15	35	+133
Aerospace	14	26	+ 86
Miscellaneous durables	37	66	+ 78
Instruments	12	21	+ 75
Machinery	86	131	+ 52
Petroleum	68	99	+ 46
Fabricated metals	20	29	+ 45
Food and beverages	71	95	+ 34
Chemicals	72	96	+ 33
Paper	50	66	+ 32
Nonferrous metals	37	46	+ 24
Textiles	58	67	+ 16
Electrical machinery	57	64	+ 12
Iron and steel	193	215	+ 11
Miscellaneous nondurables	24	25	+ 4
Autos and trucks	88	74	− 16
Nonmanufacturing:			
Electric utilities	203	370	+ 82
Communications	404	569	+ 41
Mining	84	116	+ 38
Gas utilities	23	26	+ 13
Railroads	31	34	+ 10
Airlines	54	55	+ 2
Miscellaneous transportation	70	66	− 6
Trade	702	663	− 6
Total	2,509	3,156	+ 26

Source: *Business Week,* May 26, 1973, p. 27.

Table 11

ESTIMATED COMPLIANCE COSTS OF OSHA NOISE STANDARDS, BY INDUSTRY
($ millions)

Industry	85 dbA (proposed)	90 dbA (existing)
Utilities	$ 6,300	$ 3,200
Nonelectrical machinery	4,200	1,400
Fabricated metal products	3,200	1,100
Transportation equipment	2,900	1,100
Textile mill products	2,700	1,100
Food and kindred products	2,600	590
Electrical machinery	2,300	780
Primary metals	1,900	900
Chemicals and allied products	1,400	1,100
Printing and publishing	1,000	870
Lumber and wood products	650	150
Furniture and fixtures	580	190
Stone, clay and glass	520	290
Paper and allied products	500	140
Rubber and plastic products	500	302
Petroleum and coal products	260	210
Tobacco	90	48
Apparel and related products	10	0
Leather and leather products	8	0
Total	$31,618	$13,470

Source: Bolt, Beranek and Newman, Inc., reported in *Business Week*, July 20, 1974, p. 28.

put (the "opportunity cost"). As Paul McCracken has stated the matter: "resources used in one direction are then not available to be used elsewhere. Whether they should be so used, therefore, depends not only on whether the intended use is 'good,' but on whether it is better than the uses to which the resources would otherwise be put." [25] In that spirit it should be noted that for many industries the time lost

---

[25] McCracken, "Will There Be Economics in 2024?" *University of Michigan Business Review*, September 1974, p. 13.

due to illnesses and injuries off the job far exceeds that due to on-the-job hazards. The medical director of Exxon, for example, states that non-job-related diseases and injuries account for about 96 percent of the time lost due to disability.[26] Assuming these figures are typical for industry in general, the expensive OSHA-mandated efforts apply to approximately 4 percent of disability-caused absenteeism.

Announcement Effect

One unmeasurable impact of federal regulation is the "announcement effect." For many years economists have noted the existence of this effect in the field of government spending or taxation. Thus, potential government contractors may start preparing to bid on a project before Congress has appropriated the funds, or consumers may increase their expenditures as soon as a tax cut is voted on or even while it is being considered.

Anticipated changes in governmental regulatory programs may stimulate somewhat similar responses. In Illinois, the very rumor that the Occupational Safety and Health Administration might impose more stringent standards for migrant worker housing caused straw-berry farmers to reduce their production. Lester Pitchford, the largest grower in the Centralia area, was quoted as saying, "We don't know if OSHA is coming or not, but when it was even rumored, it put it [strawberry production] out." [27] The basis for the concern was the possibility that farmers would have to provide migrant workers with the same amenities as permanent workers—100 square feet of living space (the present state standard is 60 square feet), flush toilets and showers in each room. Apparently at least some Illinois strawberry farmers concluded that the capital investment required could not be justified for a two-week harvest. According to James Mills, an official with the Illinois Department of Public Health, a basic problem is the lack of distinction under OSHA regulations between long-term and short-term migratory farm worker housing. Centralia farmers, he was quoted as saying, "just can't compete and, if OSHA puts the pressure on them, they'll get out of the migrant business completely and go strictly U-Pick" [28]—that is, where consumers pick the fruit for their own use for a fee.

---

[26] N. J. Roberts, M.D., "Medicine at Work," *The Lamp*, Fall 1974, p. 21.

[27] Pamela Meyer, "Fear of OSHA Making Farmers Plow Under Strawberry Crops," *St. Louis Post-Dispatch*, June 11, 1974, p. 7C.

[28] Ibid.

Outlook

It is noteworthy that congressional interest is mounting in legislation which would require an "economic impact" statement to be published in conjunction with the promulgation of any new regulatory standard. Several bills introduced in the 93d Congress would institute this requirement in the case of the occupational safety and health program. One approach (H.R. 9030 and S. 1147) would require OSHA to estimate the total costs a new regulation would impose upon employers.[29] A more vigorous requirement would require a showing that the benefits of the proposed standard justified the cost.[30] These bills also would allow an employer to use equipment and procedures other than those specified in a standard if such equipment afforded adequate protection to employees and did not create new hazards. In addition, some of these bills would provide for consultative inspections without the compulsory penalties required under existing law.

Yet the trend toward more intensive and more expensive job safety and health regulation is likely to continue. OSHA recently assigned a social scientist to explore the idea of extending occupational health surveillance to management personnel, supposedly to consider psychological stress among executives![31] Moreover, the National Institute for Occupational Safety and Health has recommended that it test and certify all personal protective equipment, thus excluding competent private laboratories from the testing process. The institute's proposal also calls for an "absolute guarantee" that a product it had tested would not fail in the marketplace.[32] Industry representatives are opposing both recommendations.

The future thus appears filled with more costly types of governmental encroachment upon industrial production in the United States.

---

[29] H.R. 9030, introduced by Representative Esch, and S. 1147, introduced by Senator Dominick and twenty-nine co-sponsors.

[30] H.R. 10200, introduced by Representative Beard, and S. 2823, introduced by Senator Chiles.

[31] "Boardroom Blues," *Business Week*, June 22, 1974, p. 38.

[32] "Safety Testing Plan Called Unwarranted," *NAM Reports*, July 29, 1974, p. 4.

6

HIGHER COSTS OF GOVERNMENT PURCHASES

Businessmen and scholars will continue to debate the desirability of companies' becoming more "socially responsible" (however that term is defined), but the debate may be largely over for an important sector of the American economy. In the case of the many companies that do business with the federal government, the very act of signing the procurement contract constitutes an agreement to perform a large number of "socially responsible" actions. These actions range from favoring a wide variety of disadvantaged groups to showing concern for the quality of life and the environment.

The magnitude of the government's procurement outlays, along with the importance of these outlays to many firms, creates opportunities for implementing a host of diverse economic and social aims through the contract mechanism. Thus the federal government requires that firms doing business with it maintain "fair" employment practices, provide "safe" and "healthful" working conditions, pay "prevailing" wages, refrain from polluting the air and water, give preference to American products in their purchases, and promote the rehabilitation of prisoners and the severely handicapped. Table 12 contains a sample listing of the ancillary duties required of government contractors. The concern of this study is the important extent to which these required "social responsibilities" increase the costs of the goods and services which government agencies, as well as others, purchase from the private sector.

Historical Development of Required Social Responsibility

One of the earliest attempts to bring about social change through the government procurement process was the enactment of the Eight-

Table 12

SPECIAL SOCIAL AND ECONOMIC RESTRICTIONS ON GOVERNMENT CONTRACTORS

Program	Purpose
Improve Working Conditions	
Walsh-Healey Act	Prescribes minimum wages, hours, age, and work conditions for supply contracts
Davis-Bacon Act	Prescribes minimum wages, benefits, and work conditions on construction contracts over $2,000
Service Contract Act of 1968	Extends the Walsh-Healey and Davis-Bacon Acts to service contracts
Convict Labor Act	Prohibits employment on government contracts of persons imprisoned at hard labor
Favor Disadvantaged Groups	
Equal Employment Opportunity (Executive Orders 11246 and 11375)	Prohibits discrimination in government contracting
Employment Openings for Veterans (Executive Order 11598)	Requires contractors to list suitable employment openings with state employment systems
Prison-Made Supplies (18 U.S. Code 4124)	Requires mandatory purchase of specific supplies from Federal Prison Industries, Inc.
Blind-Made Products (41 U.S. Code 46-48)	Requires mandatory purchase of products made by blind and other handicapped persons
Small Business Act	Requires "fair" portion of subcontracts to be placed with small businesses
Labor Surplus Area Concerns (32A Code of Federal Regulations 33)	Requires preference to subcontractors in areas of concentrated unemployment or underemployment
Favor American Companies	
Buy American Act	Provides preference for domestic materials over foreign materials
Preference to U.S. Vessels (10 U.S. Code 2631; 46 U.S. Code 1241)	Requires shipment of all military goods and at least half of other government goods in U.S. vessels

Program	Purpose
Protect the Environment and Quality of Life	
Clean Air Act of 1970	Prohibits contracts to a company convicted of criminal violation of air pollution standards
Care of Laboratory Animals (ASPR 7-303.44)	Requires humane treatment by defense contractors in use of experimental or laboratory animals
Humane Slaughter Act (7 U.S. Code 1901-1906)	Limits government purchases of meat to suppliers who conform to humane slaughter standards
Promote Other Government Objectives	
Embargo on Ships Engaged in Cuban and North Vietnam Trade (ASPR 1-1410)	Prohibits defense contractors from shipping supplies on foreign flag vessels that have called on Cuban or North Vietnamese ports
Use of Government Facilities (ASPR 7-104.37)	Requires defense contractors to purchase jewel bearings from government facility
Use of Government Stockpile (ASPR 1-327)	Requires defense contractors to purchase aluminum from national stockpile

Source: Murray L. Weidenbaum, "Social Responsibility Is Closer Than You Think," *University of Michigan Business Review*, July 1973.

Hour Laws, a series of statutes which established standards for hours of work. In 1892, the eight-hour workday was first extended to workers employed by contractors and subcontractors engaged in federal projects.[1] President Theodore Roosevelt, by an executive order issued in 1905, prevented the use of convict labor on government contracts. This order was based on an 1887 statute prohibiting the hiring out of convict labor.

The use of the government contract mechanism to promote social and economic objectives became widespread during the depression of the 1930s. In the face of high unemployment and depressed wages, Congress enacted the Buy American Act and most of the labor standards legislation that today governs public contracts, including the Davis-Bacon Act and the Walsh-Healey Public Contracts Act.

---

[1] These statutes have been superseded by the Work Hours Act of 1962, 76 Stat. 357. See Murray L. Weidenbaum, "Social Responsibility Is Closer Than You Think," *University of Michigan Business Review*, July 1973, pp. 32-35.

Subsequently, economic mobilization during World War II gave rise to executive orders requiring nondiscrimination in employment by government contractors and the Korean War led to a provision encouraging the placement of government contracts and subcontracts in areas of substantial labor surplus. These wartime measures were justified by the need to encourage maximum use of the nation's scarce manpower and other resources.

Rarely have these socially motivated provisions been eliminated or scaled down, even when the original conditions justifying them were no longer present. Rather, the trend has been to extend their application. In 1964, for example, an amendment to the Davis-Bacon Act broadened the prevailing wage concept to include certain fringe benefits as well as actual wages.[2] The Service Contract Act of 1965 extended to service employees of contractors the wage and labor standard policies established by the Davis-Bacon Act and the Walsh-Healey Public Contracts Act. In 1969, the Contract Hours Standards Act was amended to give the secretary of labor authority to promulgate safety and health standards for workers on government construction contracts.

In the area of energy conservation, federal contractors are being compelled to follow measures which remain voluntary for all other companies. These restrictions include holding heating levels in buildings and facilities to 68 degrees and reducing indoor lighting standards.

The federal procurement process has been utilized as the cutting edge of the effort to reduce barriers to the employment of minority groups. Since 1970, the hiring of apprentices and trainees has been required on federal construction projects. Since 1971, all government contractors and subcontractors have been required to list job openings with state employment service offices.[3] (This was especially intended to help Vietnam veterans reenter civilian labor markets.) The Vocational Rehabilitation Act of 1973 extended the equal employment opportunity programs of government contractors to handicapped personnel.

Disadvantages and Shortcomings

The advantages of using government contracts to promote basic social policies are quite clear. Important national objectives may be fostered

---

[2] Public Law 88-349, 78 Stat. 238.

[3] *Weekly Compilation of Presidential Documents*, vol. 376 (1970), article 3, section B4; Executive Order 11598, 3 CFR 161 (Supp. 1971).

without the need for additional, direct appropriations from the Treasury. To a congressman, this may seem a painless and simple approach. Restrictive procurement provisions appear to be costless and, for this reason, the government has been using them increasingly.[4] Any disadvantages, being more indirect, receive less attention. Yet, upon reflection, all of these special provisions must be seen as burdens on the governmental procurement process. They necessarily increase the overhead expenses of private contractors and federal procurement offices alike. Moreover, many of them exert upward pressure on the direct costs incurred by the government.

Supposedly, the basic concern of the government's buyers is to meet public needs at lowest cost. Yet, to take one example, the Davis-Bacon Act tends to increase the cost of public construction projects through government stipulation of wage rates higher than those that would result if the market were allowed to operate without impediment.[5] Several studies have demonstrated this effect of the Davis-Bacon Act. The act directs the Department of Labor to set "minimum" rates for construction workers on these projects. Although the law stipulates that the minimums are to be set at the level prevailing in "the city, town, village or other civil subdivision of the state in which the work is performed," in practice these rates are never the average of those paid to all construction workers in the area. Rather, "minimum" wage rates set under the Davis-Bacon provision are almost always at least as high as the local union rates and, in some instances, higher. Contractors who want to bid on these projects must agree to pay at least these rates. Professor Yale Brozen of the University of Chicago has reported that, in many cases, the Labor Department has set "minimum" rates that are above the union scale found in the area in which the work is performed. Higher union rates prevailing in some other area, as much as fifty or seventy-five miles from where the work is to be done, are frequently used instead of the local rates, despite the instruction in the law to the contrary. Indeed, Brozen found that the Labor Department, in stipulating prevailing rates, used union rates from a county other than that in which the work was done more than 50 percent of the time.[6]

In one case, for example, Davis-Bacon minimum wage rates in western Pennsylvania were based on the Pittsburgh construction

---

[4] See *Report of the Commission on Government Procurement*, vol. 1 (1972), pp. 110-24.

[5] John P. Gould, *Davis-Bacon Act* (Washington, D. C.: American Enterprise Institute, 1971).

[6] Yale Brozen, "The Law That Boomeranged," *Nation's Business*, April 1974, pp. 71-72.

union scale. The common labor rate for building construction in Pittsburgh was $6.75 an hour plus 80 cents in fringe benefits, whereas the prevailing wage for common labor in depressed Appalachia was $3.00 an hour. As a consequence, local contractors did not bid for water, sewage, and school projects in Appalachia. The "minimums" forced on them for these projects would have raised their wage scales so high that they would have been unable to compete for nongovernmental projects.[7]

The coverage of the Davis-Bacon Act is not limited to construction projects financed by federal agencies. Typically the act's requirements are appended to various programs of federal aid to state and local governments, ranging from airports to highways to libraries. Even in the case of general revenue sharing—whose basic purpose was to shift decision making from Washington to the grassroots—the law requires that all state and local governments abide by Davis-Bacon requirements for construction projects where revenue-sharing money covers one-fourth or more of the cost. This clause, not part of the original revenue-sharing bill, was attached in a rider adopted prior to passage.

Extensive studies by the General Accounting Office have shown that the Davis-Bacon Act adds from 5 to 15 percent to the cost of federal construction. During a brief period in 1971 when the President suspended the Davis-Bacon Act, several construction contracts were awarded which provide comparative data on costs with and without the influence of this piece of federal regulation.

—On a contract to install government-supplied generators in a veterans hospital, the first low bid, using the "prevailing" wage determination procedure of Davis-Bacon, was $28,884. After the suspension of Davis-Bacon, the contract was rebid. The new low bid, submitted by the original low bidder, was $22,769. The work was completed at this price for a 22 percent saving.

—A federally assisted hospital being built in the northeast United States let a contract during the suspension period for one phase of the construction. The work was completed at a 23 percent saving over the cost of a similar, earlier phase which had been subject to Davis-Bacon requirements.

—In Florida, a contractor submitted two bids for the same work on a public housing project, the higher one under the Davis-Bacon procedure and the lower one without the restriction. The difference was $18,000—or 6 percent saving.

[7] Ibid., p. 72.

—In the Midwest, an electrical company was awarded two separate contracts for similar-sized phases of work on a college building being built with federal support. The phase that was not subject to Davis-Bacon cost 10 percent less than the phase that was.[8]

Many of the special provisions imbedded in the government procurement process reflect the notions of an earlier age. For instance, the prohibition against convict labor was enacted because of concern over "chain gang" workers, a live public issue several decades ago. Changing attitudes on rehabilitation since then have cast doubt on the validity of the negative approach. In fact, under another, more recent statute, federal prisoners may work for pay in local communities under work release programs.

The greatest disadvantage of using government contracts to foster economic and social aims unrelated to the purpose of the contracts is the cumulative impact this practice has on the companies themselves. It should not be surprising that government-oriented corporations, forced to shoulder so many of the concerns and attitudes of government agencies, have come to show many of the negative characteristics of government bureaus and arsenals. In the process, much of the innovation, risk-bearing, and efficiency so characteristic of competitive enterprise may be lost to the public and private sectors alike. That would be a high price to pay for legislating social responsibility.

Adverse Effects on Defense Production

Some appreciation of the adverse consequence of government's requiring "social responsibility" from private firms can be gained from examining the industry where government control over production is most intensive and of longest standing—the defense industry. In its dealings with companies or divisions of companies that primarily serve the military market, the Department of Defense has gradually assumed decision-making functions that are normally the prerogatives of business management. In these business enterprises, a new type of relationship has been created in which the military establishment, as the buyer, makes numerous management decisions about policy and detailed procedures, decisions that in commercial business would be made by the companies themselves.[9]

---

[8] Chamber of Commerce of the United States, *Why Davis-Bacon Must Go* (Washington, D. C., n.d.), p. 1.
[9] See Murray L. Weidenbaum, *Economics of Peacetime Defense* (New York: Praeger Publishers, 1974), Chapter 6.

The government's involvement in the decision making of defense contractors takes three major forms: First, the government virtually determines the choice of products the firms produce. By awarding billions of dollars in contracts for research and development (R&D) each year, the Department of Defense strongly influences decisions about which new products its contractors will design and produce. The government as customer thus directly finances the R&D efforts and assumes much of the risk of success or failure of new product development. In the commercial economy, in contrast, R&D costs are borne not by the buyer, but by the seller, who only recovers his investment if it results in the sale of profitable products.

Second, the government also affects the way in which a company finances its operation. The Defense Department, calling upon its vast financial resources, supplies much of the plant and equipment and working capital used by its major contractors for defense work. Military contractors hold over $8 billion of outstanding "progress" payments (government payments made prior to completion of the contract and while the work is still in progress).

The third, most pervasive way in which the military establishment assumes the decision-making functions of its contractors is by closely supervising their internal operations. The military procurement regulations require private suppliers to accept, on a "take it or leave it" basis, many standard clauses in their contracts which give the governmental contracting and surveillance officers numerous powers over internal company operations. The authority assumed by the governmental "customer" includes power to review and veto company decisions about which activities to perform in-house and which to subcontract, which firms to use as subcontractors, which products to buy domestically and which to import, what internal financial reporting systems to establish, what type of industrial engineering and planning system to utilize, what minimum as well as average wage rates to pay, how much overtime work to authorize, and so forth. Thus, when a business firm enters into a contract to produce weapon systems for the military, the firm tends to take on a quasi-public nature. This is given implicit recognition by requiring the firm to conduct itself in many ways as a governmental agency, to follow the same Buy American, equal employment, depressed area, prevailing wage, and similar statutes.

The following is just a sample of the kinds of authority over private contractors which the Armed Services Procurement Regulation gives to the military contract administration office:

(1) review the contractor's compensation structure,
(2) review the contractor's insurance plans,
(3) determine the allowability of costs,
(4) negotiate overhead rates,
(5) manage special bank accounts,
(6) review, approve or disapprove and maintain surveillance of the contractor's procurement system,
(7) consent to the placement of subcontracts,
(8) monitor the contractor's financial condition,
(9) screen, redistribute and dispose of contractor inventory,
(10) evaluate contractor's requests for facilities,
(11) monitor compliance with labor and industrial relations matters,
(12) remove material from strikebound contractor's plants upon instructions from the contracting officer,
(13) review the adequacy of the contractor's traffic operations,
(14) review and evaluate preservation, packaging, and packing,
(15) provide surveillance of design, development, and production engineering efforts,
(16) review engineering studies, designs, and proposals,
(17) review test plans,
(18) evaluate the adequacy of engineering data,
(19) monitor value engineering programs,
(20) evaluate and perform surveillance of configuration management systems and procedures,
(21) evaluate the management, planning, scheduling, and allocation of engineering resources,
(22) evaluate and monitor reliability and maintainability programs,
(23) perform quality assurance,
(24) maintain surveillance of flight operations,
(25) assure compliance with safety requirements,
(26) assure compliance with small business and labor surplus area mandatory subcontracting,
(27) administer the defense industrial security program, and
(28) assure timely submission of required reports.[10]

It is hard not to conclude that the current environment for defense work attenuates the normal entrepreneurial characteristics that are associated with private enterprise. It is not surprising there-

---

[10] Excerpts from Section 1-406 of the Armed Services Procurement Regulation, as cited in Seymour Melman, *Pentagon Capitalism* (New York: McGraw-Hill, 1970), pp. 38-42.

fore that the design and production of weapon systems for the military establishment have been frequently characterized by cost overruns, technical shortcomings, and delays. The most recent and comprehensive report on this subject was made by the General Accounting Office in late 1973. The report covered forty-five major weapon systems with a total cost currently estimated in excess of $125 billion—hardly a small or unrepresentative sample. When the forty-five projects first went into development, it was estimated that they would cost $107.6 billion. Since then estimated costs have increased by $22.3 billion—an average overrun of over 20 percent. To offset this cost increase, the size of some of these programs was reduced to yield a saving of $4.8 billion, producing a net increase of $17.4 billion.[11]

Between 1957 and 1970, the Department of Defense cancelled eighty-one major weapon projects on which it had already spent a total of $11.8 billion (see Table 13). Three of the projects had already cost the nation more than $1 billion each prior to cancellation—the Air Force's manned observation laboratory, the Air Force's B-70 bomber, and the Navy's Regulus II missile. The Pentagon maintains that many of the cancelled programs contributed to the knowledge subsequently employed in weapon systems that did become operational. Yet it is hard to avoid the conclusion that a great deal of taxpayer money was wasted.

Table 13

MAJOR MILITARY PROJECTS TERMINATED, 1957–70

Category	Number	Amount Spent ($ millions)
Missile projects	28	$ 5,167
Aircraft projects	24	3,874
Space vehicle projects	2	1,897
Ordnance and other projects	27	838
Total	81	$11,776

Source: U.S. Congress, Senate, Committee on Armed Services, *Hearings on S. 939*, 92d Congress, 1st session (1971), Part 4, pp. 3006-3007.

[11] Comptroller General of the United States, *Financial Status of Selected Major Weapon Systems*, Report B-163058, November 13, 1973, p. 3.

7

HIGHER COSTS OF PERSONNEL

In a great variety of ways, federal law is increasing the cost of hiring and maintaining the work force required in the private production of goods and services. Federally mandated fringe benefits are the most obvious examples. Other costly federal influences range from controls over hiring to compulsory benefit payments to pregnant employees.

Federally Mandated Fringe Benefits

These benefits, a major example of legislation leading to higher product costs, have grown enormously since World War II. In the 1950–72 period, their cost to employers rose from a little under $4 billion to almost $35 billion, an increase of 765 percent in twenty-two years. By far the largest portion of these legally required fringe benefits is social security (old age, survivors, and disability insurance). Congress continues to enlarge this program, most recently in 1974 when it increased benefits by 11 percent. Two other programs, unemployment insurance and workman's compensation, cost employers about $5 billion each and are important but much smaller categories (see Table 14).

   The point being made here is not that these social programs are undesirable but rather that they have a significant hidden economic impact. In a very real sense, these federally mandated benefits add to the employer's cost of labor, and are then reflected in the selling price of the goods or service the firm provides or shifted backward to the employee in the form of lower direct wage payments than would otherwise be the case. These costs have grown at a faster rate than direct wages and salaries, rapidly increasing private firms' costs associated with labor. In 1950, the employers' share of legally

Table 14
COST TO PRIVATE EMPLOYERS OF REQUIRED FRINGE BENEFITS
($ in millions)

Category	1950	1955	1960	1965	1969	1970	1971	1972
Old age, survivors, and disability insurance[a]	1,590	3,133	5,947	8,717	16,767	16,954	18,982	21,484
Hospital insurance	—	—	—	—	2,252	2,276	2,437	2,761
Unemployment compensation[b]	1,473	1,550	2,823	3,729	3,381	3,482	3,692	5,500
Workman's compensation	746	1,051	1,590	2,027	4,055	4,267	4,493	4,936
Cash sickness compensation	7	5	8	9	19	27	38	45
Total	3,816	5,739	10,368	14,482	26,474	27,006	29,642	34,726
Private wages and salaries	124,300	175,100	277,100	289,600	405,568	426,875	449,338	493,605
Required fringe benefits as % of wages and salaries	3.07	3.27	3.74	5.00	6.53	6.33	6.60	7.04

a Includes railroad retirement.
b Includes railroad unemployment insurance.

Source: U.S. Department of Commerce, *Business Statistics, 1971*, p. 7; *Survey of Current Business*, July 1973, pp. 27, 33; Chamber of Commerce of the United States, *Employee Benefits, 1971* (Washington, 1972), pp. 27, 31.

required fringe benefits was just over 3 percent of wages and salaries; fifteen years later, in 1965, the figure was 5 percent; and in the following seven years the required payments rose to slightly over 7 percent.

Under some circumstances, the cost of government-mandated fringe benefits may not be fully passed on to the customer but be borne instead by labor in the form of lower wage rates than would otherwise be paid. To that extent, the higher incomes for social security recipients, as well as the various payments for other required social programs, are financed by lower real incomes for current workers.

The figures in Table 14 reflect only the part of government-mandated fringe benefits which is paid directly by the employer. They do not include the amounts deducted from the paychecks of employees as their contributions to social security and to the other social insurance programs. These personal deductions amounted to $31.9 billion in 1972, 32 percent higher than in 1969.[1] Some part of these personal deductions may be compensated by higher salaries to employees and therefore passed on to the consumer.

These required payments by both employers and employees are in addition to private pension and welfare funds. Payments into these private funds, also a substantial cost to employers, totaled over $30.6 billion in 1972.[2]

The hidden effects of the legally required fringe benefits are actually twofold. As discussed above, they increase the prices of goods and services to consumers because of higher labor costs to employers. In addition, the inflated labor costs resulting from increasingly expensive mandatory benefits may encourage firms to substitute machinery or other capital for workers when possible, thereby decreasing the demand for labor.

The upward trend of these federally mandated personnel costs is likely to continue. For example, most of the current national health insurance proposals, both Democratic and Republican versions, would assign the largest part of the cost to employers in the form of compulsory payments to health insurance carriers. Further, recent court decisions have expanded the coverage of existing federally mandated fringe benefits. Thus, in July 1974 a federal court ruled that women workers on forced maternity leave are entitled to unemployment compensation benefits.[3]

---

[1] *Survey of Current Business*, July 1973, p. 33.

[2] Ibid.

[3] "Courts Rule on Pay for Maternity Leave," *Industry Week*, August 5, 1974, p. 13.

The Federal Government and Personnel Practices

Unconcern with the importance of employee productivity is often evident in the statements of federal officials involved in the regulation of personnel practices. Speaking to a group of commercial bankers in February 1974, the deputy director of the equal opportunity program of the U.S. Treasury Department outlined a ten-point "overall strategy for identifying and correcting EEO problems." The tenth point was: "Refuse promotions or substantial wage increases to those who do not produce satisfactory EEO results, *no matter what other performance results they achieve.*" [4] In striking contradiction, the ninth point recognized a variety of important objectives: "Make each line manager and personnel manager accountable for, and rewarded in terms of, equal employment opportunity results in his or her unit *as well as other performance measures.*" [5]

In a departure from considerations of equity, EEOC Chairman John H. Powell, Jr., bluntly states that the commission is going after the nation's largest and most visible corporations. In his words, "once we get the big boys, the others will soon fall in line." [6] The irony is that the large national corporations often have the best civil rights records in industry. At the time that General Motors was being sued by the EEOC, its work force was 17 percent black and 15 percent female. According to commission member Colston A. Lewis, "Sears has the best damn affirmative action program of any company in the country. . . . The Commission is harrassing Sears and GM, because this is the way the chairman can get headlines." [7]

Many large companies, apparently viewing adverse publicity as too high a price to pay for ultimate vindication in the courts, seem to have chosen the practical course of acceding to the commission's demands. The resulting agreements often commit the companies to specific hiring quotas. Thus in 1974, nine major steel companies agreed to fill one-half of the openings in trade and craft jobs with minority and women employees.

Chairman Powell seems unmoved by arguments over reverse discrimination: "Such terms as 'quotas' and 'reverse discrimination' are merely shibboleths designed to confuse the issue." [8] But com-

---

[4] Inez S. Lee, *Current EEO Regulations,* a speech to the Pennsylvania Bankers Association, Philadelphia, February 20-21, 1974, p. 12 (emphasis added).

[5] Ibid. (emphasis added).

[6] Gerald R. Rosen, "Industry's New Watchdog in Washington," *Dun's Review,* June 1974, p. 83.

[7] Ibid.

[8] Ibid., p. 84.

mission member Colston Lewis, a southern black, is irate at the idea of forcing companies to hire less qualified workers to fill minority quotas: "It is wrong to force companies to hire unqualified applicants just because they are minority people. In the end, such practices will only serve to hurt the minorities."[9]

Judging from the EEOC's statements, the only way a company can completely satisfy the commission is to see to it that its work force reflects the minority group distribution in the areas where its plants are located. Commissioner Ethel Walsh states: "Each plant should reflect the percentages of minority people that make up the labor force in its locality."[10] A plant in Alaska should employ a high percentage of Eskimos, a plant in Oklahoma a high proportion of Indians.

This is, of course, a strategy that could backfire. A company could avoid the entire problem by locating its new plants in largely white communities. In this event, minority group applicants would have more difficulty obtaining jobs, and EEOC policy would have ended up hurting the very people it was trying to help. There is some evidence to support this concern.

Reportedly the St. Louis office of the EEOC is following standards which, whatever their intention, serve to discourage prospective employers from locating in the central city, where most of the area's black population resides. This situation results from the EEOC having established a county (not a metropolitan area) standard whereby it will infer that discrimination has taken place if a firm's work force contains a smaller percentage of blacks than reside in the county as a whole. Thus, if a company locates within the city limits of St. Louis (where the population is about 42 percent black), the constraints on its hiring practices are far more severe than if it locates in suburban St. Louis County (16 percent black).

Not too surprisingly, the opposition to the EEOC standard is led not by suburban residents but by two St. Louis city aldermen who contend that the policy will contribute to the exodus of business to the suburbs. One of them spelled out some of the reasons: "[O]nce the inference of discrimination is made, EEOC investigates further. Thousands of dollars in legal fees and personnel hours are required by the company and this is a tremendous financial drain."[11]

---

9 Ibid.

10 Ibid., p. 85.

11 Marsha Canfield, "U.S. Minority Hiring Guides Here Called Unfair," *St. Louis Globe-Democrat*, December 1, 1973.

A basic problem encountered in the administration of any national regulatory program involves the inevitable shortcomings that result from a clerical-minded, do-it-by-the-numbers approach. In the case of the Equal Employment Opportunity Program, this would appear to be a key problem in terms of both substantive issues and detailed administration.

The overhead costs associated with the Equal Employment Opportunity Program, and notably the paperwork burden, appear to be rising steadily. In July 1974, the U.S. Department of Labor gave final approval to its Revised Order No. 14 on the procedures federal agencies must use in evaluating affirmative action programs by government contractors.[12] Under this order, all prime contractors or subcontractors who have fifty or more employees and a contract of $50,000 or more are required to develop written affirmative action programs for each of their establishments. They must list each job title as it appears in their union agreements or payroll records, rather than listing only by job group, as was formerly required. The job titles must be listed from the lowest paid to the highest paid within each department or other similar organizational unit.

Further, if there are separate work units or lines of progression within a department, separate lists must be provided for each such unit, or line, including unit supervisors. For lines of progression, the order of jobs in the line through which an employee can move to the job must be indicated. If there are no formal progression lines or usual promotional sequences, job titles must be listed by departments, by job families, or by disciplines—and in order of wage rates or salary ranges. For each job title, two breakdowns are required— the total number of male and female incumbents and the total number of male and female incumbents in each of the following groups: blacks, Spanish-surnamed Americans, American Indians, and Orientals.

The order also requires listing of the wage rate or salary range for each job group at the facility, along with an explanation if minorities or women are currently being underutilized in any group. Underutilization means "having fewer minorities or women in a particular job group than would reasonably be expected by their availability." Separate utilization analyses must be prepared for minorities and women.

Clearly these requirements will necessitate a significant increase in the amount and costs of record keeping and reporting required of federal contractors.

---

[12] "Revised Order No. 14 Clarifies Rules," *NAM News*, July 29, 1974, p. 5.

Future Trends—Employee Testing

An indication of the shape of things to come may be obtained from an examination of a draft of the proposed *Uniform Guidelines on Employee Selection Procedures* which has been prepared by the U.S. Equal Employment Opportunity Coordinating Council. The purpose of the proposed guidelines is to ensure that selection procedures, in both the public and the private sectors, do not discriminate against any group on the basis of race, color, religion, sex or national origin.[13]

Although the objective is commendable, the method of carrying it out has been strongly questioned. Division fourteen of the American Psychological Association, representing about 1,300 psychologists specializing in research and its application in business and industry, has stated:

> . . . as presently constituted, the guidelines would discourage selection research because on many points the standards are unclear, unworkable, unnecessarily negative, and, in places, technically unsound. Adoption of the current draft could, therefore, result in more unfair discrimination, rather than less, and result in less effective use of the nation's human resources.[14]

The statement of the practicing psychologists might seem unusually strong. However, inspection of the proposed regulation reveals an unusually high degree of rigidity. The section on validity of personnel tests states in part:

> Under no circumstances will the general reputation of a selection procedure, its author or its publisher, or casual reports of its validity or practical usefulness be accepted in lieu of evidence of validity. Specifically ruled out are . . . data bearing on the frequency of a procedure's usage; testimonial statements and credentials of sellers, users, or consultants' and other nonempirical or anecdotal accounts of selection practices or selection outcomes.[15]

In the words of the statement of the industrial psychologists, "The pervasive problem in this draft is the attempt to specify a universally

---

[13] U.S. Equal Employment Opportunity Coordinating Council, *Uniform Guidelines on Employee Selection Procedures,* June 24, 1974, p. 1.

[14] Cited in Ad Hoc Industry Group, *Uniform Guidelines on Employee Selection* (Washington, D. C., 1974), p. 1.

[15] Equal Opportunity Coordinating Council, *Uniform Guidelines,* pp. 6-7.

applicable set of ideal procedures. . . . To create an impossible standard is to invite evasion of and disrespect for the law." [16]

From an inspection of the draft regulations, it appears that smaller employers—unless favored with access to expensive outside help—would have great difficulty in understanding the regulations and even greater difficulty in meeting the requirements. The following bureaucratese relates to the requirement that each company demonstrate that the tests it uses are valid for the specific prospective employees to be tested:

> Evidence of validation studies conducted by other employers or in other organizations . . . will be considered acceptable when . . . there are no major differences in pertinent contextual variables which are likely to affect validity significantly, and with respect to criterion related studies, no major differences in sample composition which are likely to affect validity significantly. [Section 6 (a)]

The two paragraphs below seem to be an attempt to ease the burden on the employer by relaxing the requirements under some conditions, but the language is even more formidable:

> If a criterion-related or construct validation study is technically feasible in all other respects, but it is not technically feasible to conduct a differential prediction study when required by subparagraph 14a(5) below and the test user has conducted a validation study for the job in question which otherwise meets the requirements of paragraph 14a below, the test user may continue to use the procedure operationally until such time as a differential prediction study is feasible and has been conducted within a reasonable time after it has become feasible. [Section 8(b)]
>
> A selection procedure has criterion-related validity, for the purposes of these guidelines, when the relationship between performance on the procedure and performance on at least one relevant criterion measure is statistically significant at the .05 level of significance. . . . If the relationship between a selection procedure and a criterion measure is significant but non-linear, the score distribution should be studied to determine if there are sections of the regression curve with zero or near zero slope where scores do not reliably predict different levels of job performance. [Section 14(a) (5) (6)]

The quotations above are not isolated instances. They are indicative of the general tone of the proposed regulations. No mention

---

[16] Ad Hoc Industry Group, *Uniform Guidelines*, p. 1.

of cost or minimum size of firm or limits of practical application is even remotely hinted at anywhere in the proposal.

An ad hoc industry group consisting of representatives of leading business and professional associations (ranging from the Business Roundtable to the American Society for Personnel Administration) has warned that the proposed guidelines, if implemented, would eliminate objective test selection of employees. If this should happen, it could turn back the clock and reinstate less job-related and potentially more bias-laden procedures, such as the uncontrolled interview.[17]

Future Trends—Employee Housing

It is ironic to contemplate, but the notion of a company town is reemerging via the efforts of the U.S. Civil Rights Commission. The commission has recommended that the Office of Federal Contract Compliance require contractors and subcontractors, as a condition of eligibility for federal contracts, to demonstrate the adequacy of nondiscriminatory low- and moderate-income housing in any community in which they are located or propose to locate. The commission states:

> In the event the supply of such housing is not adequate, contractors should be required to submit affirmative action plans, including firm commitments from local government officials, housing industry representatives and civic leaders that will assure an adequate supply of such housing within a reasonable time following execution of the contract. Failure to carry out the assurance should be made grounds for cancellation of the contract and ineligibility for future government contracts.[18]

Concluding Note

It is difficult to reconcile the ambitious proposals of the Civil Rights Commission and the Equal Employment Opportunity Coordinating Council with efforts to increase productivity and minimize the costs of production in order to curb inflationary pressures. On reflection, with so many other major domestic initiatives revealing the same ignorance of their impact on costs and prices, it may not be surprising that inflation has become a major and continuing domestic problem.

---

[17] Ibid., p. 2.

[18] Taylor Pennsoneau, "New U.S. Agencies to Curb Housing Bias in Suburbs Here Urged by Rights Panel," *St. Louis Post-Dispatch*, August 12, 1974, p. 1.

8

HIGHER INTEREST RATES

The more or less unfettered expansion of Federal credit programs and the accompanying deluge of agency direct and guaranteed securities to be financed in the credit markets has undoubtedly permitted Congress and the Administration to claim the wonder of wonders—something for nothing, or almost nothing. But as with all such sleight-of-hand feats, the truth is somewhat different.

> Bruce MacLaury, president,
> Federal Reserve Bank of Minneapolis

Over the years, many credit programs have been established by the federal government. Since most of this activity does not appear in the federal budget, it seems to be a painless way of achieving national objectives. In the main, the federal government is "merely" guaranteeing private borrowing or sponsoring ostensibly private institutions, albeit with federal aid. Examples include the federal land banks and the federal home loan banks.

Yet, upon closer inspection, we find that this use of the governmental credit power results in substantial costs to the society as well as to taxpayers. In a comprehensive study of federal credit programs for the prestigious Commission on Money and Credit, for example, Warren Law of Harvard University concluded that these programs have created inflationary pressures in every year since World War II.[1]

The programs of the government-sponsored credit agencies do little to increase the total pool of capital available to the economy.

---

[1] Warren A. Law, "The Aggregate Impact of Federal Credit Programs on the Economy," in Commission on Money and Credit, *Federal Credit Programs* (Englewood Cliffs, N. J.: Prentice-Hall, 1963), p. 310.

Rather, by preempting a major portion of the annual flow of savings, they reduce the amount of credit that can be provided to unprotected borrowers (mainly consumers), state and local governments, and private business firms. During periods of tight money, it is difficult for unassisted borrowers to attract the financing they require, in part because they have to compete against the government-aided borrowers. (Federal loan guarantees reduce the risk of lending money to the insured borrowers.) The result of this uneven competition is still higher interest rates.

More detailed analysis of the phenomenon of federal credit programs is warranted.

Effects on Total Saving and Investment

While the theoretical literature on the effects of federal credit programs on the total flow of saving and investment in the American economy is ambiguous,[2] the empirical literature is clear. These programs do little if anything to increase the total flow of saving or investment. They do exert upward pressures on interest rates as investment funds are bid away from other sectors.

In commenting on borrowing by agencies of the federal government, Dr. Henry Kaufman, a distinguished economist with the investment house of Salomon Brothers, has written: "Federal agency financing does not do anything directly to enlarge the supply of savings. . . . In contrast, as agency financing bids for the limited supply of savings with other credit demanders, it helps to bid up the price of money."[3]

Dr. Bruce MacLaury points out that there are extra costs associated with introducing new government credit agencies to the capital markets. Among these costs are selling issues that are smaller than some minimum efficiently tradeable size and selling securities that only in varying degree approximate the characteristics of direct government debt in terms of perfection of guarantee, flexibility of timing and maturities, "cleanness" of instrument, et cetera. He points out that, as a result of such considerations, the market normally charges a premium over the interest cost on direct government debt of comparable maturity. That premium ranges from one-fourth of 1 percent

---

[2] Dan Larkins, *$300 Billion in Loans: An Introduction to Federal Credit Programs* (Washington, D. C.: American Enterprise Institute, 1972).

[3] Henry Kaufman, "Federal Debt Management: An Economist's View from the Marketplace," in Federal Reserve Bank of Boston, *Issues in Federal Debt Management* (Boston, 1973), pp. 171, 173.

on the issues of well-known federally sponsored agencies such as Federal National Mortgage Association to more than one-half percent on such exotics as new community bonds. He points out: "In general, if cost of financing were the only consideration, it would be most efficient to have the Treasury itself provide the financing for direct loans by issuing government debt in the market." [4]

MacLaury also describes the reduced efficiency that occurs in the economy as a result of the federal "umbrella" that is spread over many credit activities without distinguishing their relative credit risks:

> One function that credit markets are supposed to perform is that of distinguishing different credit risks and assigning appropriate risk premia. . . . [T]his is the essence of the ultimate resource-allocation function of credit markets.
>
> As an increasing proportion of issues coming to the credit markets bears the guarantee of Uncle Sam, the scope for the market to differentiate credit risks inevitably diminishes. . . . Theoretically, the Federal agencies issuing or guaranteeing debt would perform this role, charging as costs of the programs differing rates of insurance premia. In practice, all of the pressures are against such differential pricing of risks.[5]

Effects on Sectors of the Economy

In an article based on work done in the U.S. Treasury Department, the present writer pointed out: "it must be recognized that the very nature of [federal] credit assistance is to create advantages for some groups of borrowers and disadvantages for others." [6] This phenomenon occurs for a variety of reasons. The total supply of funds is broadly determined by household and business saving and the ability of banks to increase the money supply. The normal response of financial markets to an increase in the demand for funds by a borrower, such as is represented by a federal credit program, is an increase in interest rates so as to balance the demand for funds with the supply of saving. But the federal government's demand for funds are "interest-inelastic" (the Treasury will generally raise the money that it requires regardless of the interest rate), and the interest

---

[4] Bruce K. MacLaury, "Federal Credit Programs—The Issues They Raise," in *Issues in Federal Debt Management*, p. 215.

[5] Ibid., p. 217.

[6] Murray L. Weidenbaum, "Financing and Controlling Federal Credit Programs," *Federal Home Loan Bank Board Journal*, September 1971, p. 15.

elasticity of saving is relatively modest. Thus, weak and marginal borrowers will be "rationed" out of financial markets in the process, while the Treasury and other borrowers pay higher rates of interest.[7]

The literature provides clear answers to the questions: "Who will be rationed out? Who will be the new disadvantaged in the credit market?" To quote Dr. Kaufman again:

> It is unlikely to be the large well-known corporations or the U.S. Government. It is likely to be some State and local government, medium-sized and smaller businesses, some private mortgage borrowers not under the Federal umbrella, and some consumer sectors. . . . This is bound to contribute to additional economic and financial concentration in the United States.[8]

James McKeon also notes that the continued expansion of government-assisted credit "would result in corporate issuers [who do not receive federal aid] having to reach a wider market with resultant consequences for rates. It would also probably bar even more lower-rated issuers from the bond market in the years to come."[9] Kaufman contends that the substantial volume of new offerings by the federal credit agencies will widen sharply the spread between the interest rates on these issues and those of the U.S. government, while the spread between the agencies and high-grade corporate bonds will tend to be very narrow.

Thus, federal credit programs increase the cost to the taxpayer by raising the interest rate at which the Treasury borrows. These programs simultaneously cause an increase in the interest rates paid by the private sector. Although these costs do not show up in the form of federal appropriations for the activities being aided, they do tend to raise the cost of producing goods and services.

Growth of Federal Credit Programs

As shown in Table 15, there has been a massive expansion in the size and relative importance of federal government credit demands over

---

[7] Patricia F. Bowers, *Private Choice and Public Welfare* (Hinsdale, Ill.: Dryden Press, 1974), p. 496. See also Alan Greenspan, "A General View of Inflation in the United States," in *Inflation in the United States* (New York: The Conference Board, 1974), p. 4.

[8] Kaufman, "Federal Debt Management," pp. 171, 173.

[9] James J. McKeon, "Agency Debt Growth Shouldering Others from Market," *Money Manager*, December 10, 1973, p. 3. See also Bowers, *Private Choice and Public Welfare*, pp. 494-96: The "two borrowing groups most adversely affected . . . are state and local governments and small businesses."

Table 15

IMPACT ON CREDIT MARKETS OF FEDERAL AND
FEDERALLY ASSISTED BORROWING FROM THE PUBLIC

(fiscal years, $ in billions)

Category of Credit	1960	1965	1970	1971	1972
A. Net federal borrowing (budget financing)	2.2	4.0	5.4	19.5	19.4
B. Net federally assisted borrowing (financing outside of the budget) a	3.3	6.8	15.1	18.2	19.2
C. Total federal and federally assisted borrowing (A + B)	5.5	10.8	20.5	37.7	38.6
D. Total funds advanced in credit markets	43.4	69.6	89.0	120.0	145.6
(C) ÷ (D)	12.7%	15.5%	23.0%	31.4%	26.5%

a Obligations issued by government-sponsored agencies or guaranteed by federal government agencies.

Source: Federal Reserve System's flow-of-funds accounts; Treasury Department data.

the past decade. In 1960, the federal share of funds raised in private capital markets, using the Federal Reserve System's flow-of-funds data, was 12.7 percent. By 1970, the government's share had risen to 23.0 percent, and it has continued to grow since then.

Virtually every session of the Congress in recent years has enacted additional federal credit programs. Since 1960, the Federal National Mortgage Association (Fannie Mae) has been joined by General National Mortgage Association (Ginnie Mae), Student Loan Marketing Association (Sally Mae) and, most recently, the U.S. Railway Association (Fannie Rae).[10] The upward trend does not seem to have leveled off. In view of the financial problems faced by some public utilities, proposals are now being seriously advanced for federal credit guarantees of private electric utility bonds and of bank deposits by local governments.[11]

In considering proposals for new loan guarantees by the federal government, attention needs to be given to the existing burden of liabilities and contingent liabilities already borne by the U.S. Treasury.

[10] For detail see Murray L. Weidenbaum and Dan Larkins, *The Federal Budget for 1973* (Washington: American Enterprise Institute, 1972), Chapter 6.

[11] William G. Rosenberg, "Rates, Consumer Pressure, and Finance," *Public Utilities Fortnightly,* January 31, 1974, pp. 3-7.

Table 16 summarizes the major commitments of such a nature. On June 30, 1973, they totalled in excess of $1.7 trillion, of which direct liabilities were over $520 billion and government credit programs accounted for over $160 billion. By way of comparison, total federal revenues for the fiscal year 1975 are estimated at about $300 billion.

Table 16

LIABILITIES AND OTHER FINANCIAL COMMITMENTS OF THE U.S. GOVERNMENT, AS OF JUNE 30, 1973

($ millions)

Category	Applicable to Other Government Funds	Applicable to the Public	Total
Liabilities			
The public debt	124,210	333,932	458,142
Agency securities	1,996	9,113	11,109
Deposit fund liability accounts	—	3,653	3,653
Checks and other instruments outstanding	—	7,075	7,075
Accrued interest on the public debt	—	2,874	2,874
Other Treasury liabilities	—	418	418
Accounts payable on the books of government agencies	6,377	31,049	37,426
Subtotal, liabilities	132,583	388,114	520,697
Contingent Liabilities			
Government guarantees insuring private lenders against losses	—	160,713	160,713
Insurance commitments	—	1,021,915	1,021,915
Unadjudicated claims	—	5,762	5,762
International commitments	—	17,502	17,502
Subtotal, contingent liabilities	—	1,205,892	1,205,892
GRAND TOTAL	132,583	1,594,006	1,726,589

Note: Excludes actuarial deficiency in social security and other social insurance programs, as well as other contingencies specified in the source.

Source: Department of the Treasury, Bureau of Accounts, *Statement of Liabilities and Other Financial Commitments of the United States Government as of June 30, 1973,* January 1974.

Information on federal credit programs is contained in Table 17. An examination of the array of programs is enlightening. In the

Table 17
FEDERAL GOVERNMENT LOAN AND CREDIT GUARANTEES, AS OF JUNE 30, 1973
($ millions)

Department or Agency		Amount of Contingency	
	Total	For guarantees in force	For commitments to guarantee
Agriculture	$ 10,563	$ 9,442	$ 1,121
Commerce	2,639	1,320	1,319
Defense	244	244	—
Health, Education, and Welfare	2,554	2,146	408
Housing and Urban Development	109,160	102,509	6,651
Transportation	731	627	104
Agency for International Development	277	277	—
General Services Administration	684	640	44
Veterans Administration	25,372	24,420	952
Emergency Loan Guarantee Board	250	150	100
Export-Import Bank	4,576	1,784	2,792
Interstate Commerce Commission	42	42	—
National Credit Union Administration	4	4	—
Overseas Private Investment Corporation	218	191	27
Small Business Administration	3,399	2,678	721
Total	160,713	146,474	14,239

Note: Excludes government-sponsored enterprises, such as Federal National Mortgage Association, Federal Land Banks, and Federal Home Loan Banks.

Source: U.S. Department of the Treasury, Bureau of Accounts, *Statement of Liabilities and Other Financial Commitments of the United States Government as of June 30, 1973,* January 1974.

typical case, the area being aided is one subject to close federal regulation (agriculture) or has become, at least in part, a federal responsibility (housing and veterans' assistance).

Relation to Government Controls

An examination of existing programs of federal guarantee of private credit reveals how the credit assistance is often accompanied by various forms of governmental control or influence over the recipients of the credit. For example, federal credit guarantees for shipbuilders are part of a broader program whereby the federal government requires the builders to incorporate various "national defense" features into the vessels.

It is instructive to examine the largest federal program for guaranteeing private credit, that administered by the Federal Housing Administration (FHA), in order to observe the extent to which controls accompany the credit assistance. The FHA conducts an inspection of each residence to determine whether the builder has abided by all of the agency's rules and regulations governing the construction of the homes that it insures. There are four separate veto points facing a builder applying for FHA insurance of mortgages for a new project: (1) affirmative marketing to minority groups, (2) environmental impact, (3) architectural review, and (4) underwriting.

Because of the division of responsibilities among the various federal housing offices, considerable confusion and delay often arises. For example, after the underwriting has been approved, one which gives an appraised value high enough to cover the builder's costs, additional requirements may be imposed by the environmental impact office or by the architectural review which substantially raise the cost of the project. Then the builder must return to the first office and attempt to obtain a revised underwriting.

Miles Colean, a distinguished analyst of the housing industry, has noted the deleterious effects on the housing industry of the increasing array of governmental controls imposed via the FHA program: "The complications of FHA operations, by introducing numerous requirements irrelevant to the extension of mortgage credit, placed the market oriented activity of FHA at a competitive disadvantage." [12]

---

[12] Miles L. Colean, "Quarterly Economic Report," *Mortgage Banker*, March 1974, p. 63.

In October 1972, the National Center for Housing Management contracted with the U.S. Department of Housing and Urban Development to study HUD's housing programs. For its study, the center drew on a distinguished group of housing experts. In assessing the effects of the requirements which have been added in recent years to the FHA processing format—"such matters as affirmative marketing, environmental protection, and project selection"—the study concluded:

> . . . the Task Force feels that HUD has not proceeded in the most logical fashion in dealing with these new requirements. It has tended to add them on to the process without even analyzing the effect that they would have on that process. . . . The end result has been that the constant imposition of new socially useful requirements for FHA processing has produced a substantial loss of competitive status for FHA's single-family programs.[13]

Thus, in effect, the implicit federal credit subsidy to the FHA is being absorbed to a large extent by social objectives. The current cost of attempting to implement these objectives by this method may be quite high compared to more direct alternatives. Perhaps the most fundamental problem that has arisen is the fact that FHA guaranteed loans have always been subject to an officially determined mortgage interest rate ceiling. In states with low usury ceilings, this has at times either prevented otherwise eligible people from using the FHA insurance program or required the use of "points" and other complicating subterfuges.

Once an industry has become dependent on federal financial assistance, that dependence can be used to impose additional controls, controls which may be unrelated to protecting the government's investment or contingent liability. An example is a recent report on energy policy of the Joint Economic Committee of the Congress. Among various proposals, the report recommended that the Congress enact authority to require minimum standards for thermal efficiency in new building as a prerequisite for approval under any federal subsidy or mortgage insurance program.[14]

The proposal for federal guarantees of electric utility bonds is another example of the tendency for federal credit assistance to be accompanied by extensive and often costly systems of federal controls. The draft bill for the plan contains a variety of new federal

---

[13] *Report of the Task Force on Improving the Operation of Federally Insured or Financed Housing Programs* (Washington: National Center for Housing Management, Inc., n.d.), pp. 69-70.

[14] U.S. Congress, Joint Economic Committee, *A Reappraisal of the U.S. Energy Policy*, 93d Congress, 2d session (1974), pp. 2-3.

controls over the activities of electric utilities, which historically have been subject only to state control or to the discretion of company management.[15] Under the proposal, before a utility could apply for the federal guarantee, its state public utility commission would have to submit a "Statement of Need" which the Federal Power Commission deemed consistent with "national standards." Each public utility applying for a federal guarantee would have to demonstrate to the commission that no other reasonable means of financing was available on "reasonable" credit terms. The net interest cost on each utility bond issue guaranteed by the FPC could not exceed what the chairman of the FPC deemed to be reasonable. The FPC would be required to determine that the management of the utility was "efficient."

Summary

Boiled down to basics, federal guarantees of bonds issued by business and other institutions involve putting "the monkey" on someone else's back. They do not increase the amount of investment funds available to the economy. Rather, to the extent they succeed, they merely take capital funds away from other sectors of the economy and lead to similar requests for aid by those sectors. These government guarantees also tend to raise the level of interest rates in the economy, both for private and government borrowers. Thus they increase an important component of business costs.

Over the period in which an ever-increasing proportion of private saving has been absorbed on government borrowing, the inelasticity of demand of the money and capital markets has been rising. In other words, governments elbow private borrowers out of the capital markets simply because the federal government and its agencies are willing to pay whatever interest rates are required in order to acquire the capital they need. Private borrowers are restricted by competitive pressures and the limits of their own resources.

The pressure on interest rates, Alan Greenspan contends, forces the Federal Reserve System to increase the reserves of the banking system in order to supply financing to the private sector. This, in turn, contributes to the general inflationary condition of the economy.[16] Federal credit programs therefore tend to raise the private cost of production in two ways—by causing an increase in interest rates and by contributing to the situation that leads to a higher general rate of inflation.

---

[15] Proposed "Electric Utility Guarantee Act of 1974."
[16] Greenspan, "General View of Inflation," p. 4.

9

THE COST OF CONFLICTING GOVERNMENT OBJECTIVES: WHICH "GOOD" IS BETTER?

> Flood control planners, pollution control planners, site planners, land use planners, watershed planners—all have been going off in their own separate directions as if each were independent of and apart from the others, each with its own individual goals.
>
> Lester Edelman, counsel,
> House Committee on Public Works

The simple task of washing children's pajamas in New York State exemplifies how two laws can pit one worthy public objective against another—in this case ecology and safety. Because of a ban on phosphates in detergents, the mother who launders her child's sleepwear in a legally acceptable fashion risks washing away its required flame-retardant properties.

In 1973, in an effort to halt water pollution, New York State banned the sale of detergents containing phosphates. Less than two months later, a federal regulation mandating that all children's sleepwear, sizes 0 to 6X, be flame-retardant took effect across the country. New York housewives face a dilemma—because phosphate detergents are the best protector of fire-retardancy. Phosphates hold soil and minerals in solution, preventing the formation of a mask on the fabric that inactivates flame-resistance. Soap and, to a lesser degree, many non-phosphate detergents redeposit those harmful items during the wash cycle. Although flame-resistant phosphate substitutes are being tested, none has received general acceptance. We share the lament of the *New York Times:* "So what's a conscientious mother in a phosphate-banned area to do? Smuggle them in? Commit an illegal act of laundry? Risk dressing her child in nightclothes that could burn up?"[1]

A recent incident in Florida underscores the great difficulties that arise when public policy is burdened with so many varieties of compulsory "social responsibility." In the fall of 1973, Offshore Power Systems announced plans to construct a facility in the Jacksonville area to produce floating barges on which seawater-cooled nuclear reactors would later be installed. The company had worked out an affirmative-action agreement with local community groups under which it was committed to ensure that 23 percent of the 11,000 to 14,000 jobs expected to be created by the new facility would be made available to minority-group applicants. The agreement had been hailed in Jacksonville as a substantial step toward reducing the city's chronically high unemployment rate among blacks.

But the Florida Audubon Society objected to the project on the grounds that the Corps of Engineers had not addressed "the concept and feasibility" of floating nuclear plants in its environmental impact statement and had failed to analyze adequately the possibility of alternate sites. Although the community groups argued that the economic advantages would outweigh any adverse environmental effects, the district court issued a temporary restraining order blocking the project.[2]

Regulating Restrooms: A Case of Separate But Equal

Common sense seems to be in chronically short supply in the administration of governmental regulatory activities. The controversy over restrooms provides a case in point. For well-known biological reasons, the Occupational Safety and Health Administration as well as many state laws require the provision of some kind of lounge area adjacent to women's restrooms in work facilities. However, the Equal Employment Opportunity Commission has entered this ticklish area by requiring that male toilet and lounge facilities, although separate, should be equal to those provided to women. Hence, either equivalent lounges must be built adjacent to the men's toilets or the women's lounges must be dismantled, OSHA and state laws notwithstanding. One personnel supervisor has stated that employers will just have to

---

[1] Nadine Brozan, "Flame-Retardant Pajamas: An Issue of Child Safety vs. Ecology," *New York Times*, April 30, 1974, p. 42.

[2] "Audubon Society Tangles With Job-Opportunity Issue," *Public Interest Alert*, November 1, 1973, pp. 2-3.

hope that their more mischievous male employees remain ignorant of the EEOC ruling and avoid lodging official complaints.[3]

Another area of conflict among government objectives occurs in the interaction between older statutes, such as the antitrust statutes, and newer ones, such as those governing safety and the environment. For example, the utility companies once sought to ensure the safety of gas burners used for heating by supplying gas only to users whose burners had passed the necessary tests and received a safety seal. The manufacturer of one brand of burner that had failed to get a safety seal sued, claiming an antitrust violation. The court ruled that the complaint was sufficient to state a claim on which relief could be granted.[4] The same point was illustrated in another court decision, which held that "violations of antitrust laws could not be defended on the ground that a particular accused combination would not injure but would actually help manufacturers, laborers, retailers, consumers, or the public in general."[5]

In the 1960s, the automobile industry assigned engineers to find the best and most efficient way to control automobile emissions in the smog-filled Los Angeles area. There was prompt antitrust objection to a common industry-wide effort. As a result, the exchange of confidential technical data among company engineers was prohibited.[6] The result was costly duplication of effort and perhaps lost time.

The Jones Act—which requires shipments of cargo from one port in the United States to another to be made by American vessels—also illustrates the conflict between two or more objectives. The staff of the Senate Finance Committee estimates that it costs 8 to 10 cents more per million cubic feet to transport liquified natural gas (LNG) between Alaska and the West Coast by American flag vessels than by foreign flag vessels. Attempts to avoid this 8-10 cent "tax" result in a roundabout, expensive procedure whereby Alaska exports LNG to other countries and the mainland United States imports LNG from the South Pacific and Russia.[7] The Jones Act was enacted to aid the

---

[3] J. Kenneth Kriegsmann, "Pity the Poor Personnel Man," *Dun's Review*, February 1973, p. 89.

[4] Radiant Burners, Inc. v. Peoples Gas Light and Coke Co., 364 U.S. 656 (1961).

[5] Giboney v. Empire Storage and Ice Co., 376 U.S. 490, 496 (1949).

[6] Consent decree in United States v. Automobile Manufacturers Association, Inc. (1969), quoted in Robert L. Werner, *Antitrust, Social Responsibility and Changing Times*, an address to the Conference Board's Thirteenth Conference on Antitrust Issues, New York City, March 7, 1974, p. 11.

[7] U.S. Congress, Senate, Committee on Finance, *Fiscal Policy and the Energy Crisis*, 93d Congress, 1st session (1973), p. 35.

American shipping industry. In practice, it tends to aid foreign shipping industries and to reduce the availability or increase the cost of goods to the American consumer.

Another conflict between two government objectives occurred in Philadelphia, where a controversy over lead-based paint had the result of all but eliminating mortgage assistance for low-income families. The problem arose because of a court ruling that prohibited the Department of Housing and Urban Development (HUD) from selling the stock of housing it had acquired before cleansing it of lead-based paint (which can cause lead poisoning in children if they swallow enough of it). The federal government maintained that the cost of eliminating the lead-based paint was prohibitive. Hence, the government-owned houses simply sat vacant and many were vandalized beyond repair. To compound the problem, HUD instructed FHA's regional office not to guarantee any mortgages on homes unless they were certified to be free of lead-based paint. That further paralyzed the low-income housing market in Philadelphia by removing virtually all of the remaining moderately priced, inner-city dwellings from the reach of FHA's assistance programs.

The regional director of HUD summed up the situation this way: "It is a hell of a mess. Frankly, I'm not sure what's going to happen, and I don't think anyone else is either. . . . I said, it is a horrible, heart breaking, hell of a mess."[8] The interaction of the two, apparently worthy governmental objectives—safeguarding the health of the young and providing housing for the poor—was, in the words of the *New York Times*, "a chronicle crammed with ironies. . . ,"[9] in which neither objective was effectively achieved.

Who Will Regulate the Regulators?

Just as the types of business regulation have expanded, so has the variety of political and administrative bodies exercising regulatory authority. The story of Consolidated Edison's request to convert two New York City power plants back to coal is one example of the problems caused by this complexity. The conversion to coal was advocated by the Federal Energy Administration, denied by New York City's environmental protection agency, and subsequently approved by the New York state environmental agency. However, new appointees in the latter two agencies have indicated that they will

---

[8] James T. Wooten, "Lead Paint Ban Tying Up Mortgage Help for the Poor," *New York Times*, May 9, 1974, p. 1.
[9] Ibid.

reverse their predecessors, thus maintaining the contradiction. The hundreds of thousands of people in the Consolidated Edison service area who live outside of New York City have no voice in a decision which will greatly affect their jobs and well-being.

Another striking example of the same problem is the division of authority for pollution control of the Hudson River between the state authorities of New York and New Jersey. Each has jurisdiction from its own shore to the middle of the river.[10]

Spokesmen for the electric utility industry frequently complain about the multiplicity of approvals that are required before a new electric generating plant can be put into operation. The average person may discount this concern until he or she actually sees the extensive and repetitious nature of these requirements. A listing of the authorizations required for the construction and operation of a single generating plant is given in Table 18. In this case, in order to proceed with its proposed facility at Fulton, the Philadelphia Electric Company has to obtain twenty-four different kinds of approvals from five federal agencies, five state agencies, two townships, and a regional commission. The required permits and licenses range from approval of its towers by federal and state aviation agencies to authorization from the state environmental agency for a trestle across Peters Creek.

Recently an Atomic Industrial Forum survey of 95 nuclear power plant projects of 37 different utilities reported that 70 of the 95 have experienced delays ranging from 2 to 66 months. Average delays of 24.3 months were reported for plants under construction and 25.9 months for those awaiting permits. By far, the most frequently cited reason for the power plants being behind schedule was governmental licensing and regulatory requirements.[11]

The Federal Energy Administration (FEA) has urged the Congress to reduce the prolonged hearings and repetitious licensing procedures which interfere with the objective of increasing the nation's energy supplies. The FEA has also urged alteration of the dual hearings procedure which has prevailed under the concept of treating each nuclear reactor on a "one of a kind basis." [12] Presently, section 189a of the Atomic Energy Act requires a public hearing before issuance of both the construction permit and the operating license. FEA recom-

---

[10] Alfred C. Neal, *The Business-Government Relationship*, a paper presented at UCLA, January 24, 1974, p. 5.

[11] "Government Is Main Atom Plant Roadblock," *Industry Week*, May 27, 1974, p. 24.

[12] Statement by Robert H. Shatz, assistant administrator of the Federal Energy Office, before the Joint Committee on Atomic Energy at the hearings on Nuclear Power Plant Siting and Licensing, March 21, 1974, p. 5.

Table 18

GOVERNMENT AUTHORIZATIONS REQUIRED FOR CONSTRUCTION AND OPERATION OF A NUCLEAR GENERATING PLANT[a]

Agency	Nature of Authorization
Federal	
Atomic Energy Commission	Construction permit
Atomic Energy Commission	Operating license
Atomic Energy Commission	By-product material license
Atomic Energy Commission	Special nuclear materials license
Corps of Engineers	Dredging in navigable streams and tributaries permit
Corps of Engineers	Construction of structures in navigable streams and tributaries
Environmental Protection Agency	National pollution discharge elimination system permit
Federal Aviation Administration	Construction of meteorological towers
Federal Aviation Administration	Construction of cooling towers
Federal Aviation Administration	Construction of transmission towers
Department of Transportation	Authorization to transport fuel in approved containers
State	
Department of Environmental Resources	Air pollution permit for auxiliary boilers and radioactive off-gas facilities
Department of Environmental Resources	Industrial waste permit for thermal, chemical, and radioactive liquid discharges
Department of Environmental Resources	Water obstruction permit for trestle across Peters Creek
Department of Environmental Resources	Steam-encroachment permits for construction extending into the Susquehanna River
Department of Environmental Resources	Sewage permit
Department of Environmental Resources	Certification of water quality for plant water
Department of Labor and Industry	Use and occupancy permit for buildings

Agency	Nature of Authorization
Department of Transportation	Notice of construction (same as Federal Aviation Administration)
State Police-Fire Marshal	Flammable liquids permit to store and use potentially hazardous materials
Public Utility Commission	Certificate of necessity to exempt plant buildings from local zoning ordinances
Local	
Drumore Township	Building permit
Fulton Township	Building permit
Susquehanna River Basin Commission	Surface water withdrawal

a The example used is the proposed Fulton generating station of the Philadelphia Electric Company.

Source: U.S. Atomic Energy Commission, *Draft Environmental Statement Related to the Proposed Fulton Generating Station Units 1 and 2, Philadelphia Electric Company*, Dockets Nos. 50-463 and 50-464, May 1974, pp. 1-2.

mended eliminating the mandatory hearing at the construction permit stage "where no valid contested issues are raised, and no real purpose is served by a public hearing." If a hearing is held at the construction permit stage, FEA urged that it be comprehensive and thus render further hearings unnecessary unless there are changes that could significantly affect public health and safety.[13]

Representatives of the electric utilities contend that existing procedures unnecessarily delay the process of getting new power plants, especially nuclear plants, into operation. The vice chairman of Commonwealth Edison Company states that "there is no justification for continual and repetitious litigation of the same questions over and over again, and always with the same intervenors represented by the same attorneys." He urges that the pros and cons of a particular energy installation decision be reviewed "once and for all." He also estimates that delaying a power station may involve continuing costs of up to $1 million a week.[14] The multiplicity of regulatory reviews for new utility facilities and the resultant delays are, of course, one factor among several in the recent spate of utility rate increases.

---

[13] Ibid., p. 7.
[14] Gordon R. Corey, *Central Station Nuclear Electric Power in Meeting the Energy Crisis*, a lecture at the City College of New York, May 14, 1973, p. 3.

Sometimes government regulators hamstring private industry by failing to follow federal requirements, which is the situation in a still pending case involving the Kennecott Copper Corporation and the Environmental Protection Agency (EPA). In this case the lack of an EPA-approved clean-air plan for the state of Nevada delayed Kennecott from proceeding with an emissions control plan. A tentative plan was submitted in January 1972. But more than two years later the federal agency had neither approved it nor offered an alternative, as the Clean Air Act requires it to do within six months. Kennecott is going ahead with a $24 million project to clean up emissions from its Nevada smelter, hoping that ultimately it will receive the agency's approval. "It's ironic that the longer the delay in approval, the dirtier the air gets," a Kennecott spokesman was quoted as stating.[15] Kennecott has notified EPA that it plans to sue the agency for failure to obey the Clean Air Act of 1970. Such notification is required before the suit can be instituted.

One recent environment case surely must leave the business community shaking its head in wonderment. It seems to be a real-world illustration of the old gag, "Heads I win, tails you lose." A federal district judge in Texas was reported to have ordered the private developer of a community project near San Antonio to pay the attorneys' fees for four citizens' groups, even though the private developer was not even a party to the suit (the suit was filed against the federal government, which had accepted the developers' environmental impact statement) and even though the citizens' groups lost the suit! The court proclaimed the interesting doctrine that, since private citizens carry much of the burden of seeing that federal environmental policy is carried out, awarding them their costs—even if they lose—will help ensure that information concerning projects and their impact on the environment will become public (Sierra Club v. Lynn, Western District Texas).[16] Wittingly or unwittingly, such court actions tend in practice to shift the costs of private citizens' groups to the consumer as a whole—with the consumer having no voice in the matter.

Conclusion

If there is any lesson that economics has to offer, it is that difficult choices have to be made. As a nation, we cannot carry an endless

---

[15] "EPA Faces Charges That It Disobeyed the Clean Air Act," *Wall Street Journal*, May 9, 1974, p. 19.

[16] "Financing the Ecology Battle," *Business Week*, November 17, 1973, p. 87.

array of governmental responsibilities, whether they are financed via the public purse or through higher prices. The government cannot be expected to assume all sorts of new burdens without lightening some of the present load. A Vietnam TV clip comes to mind: the one that shows so many soldiers attempting to climb aboard a helicopter that the vehicle never got off the ground.

10

THE GOVERNMENTAL PRESENCE IN BUSINESS DECISION MAKING

Experience should teach us to be most on our guard to protect liberty when the Government's purposes are beneficent. Men born to freedom are naturally alert to repel invasion of their liberty by evil-minded rulers. The greatest dangers to liberty lurk in insidious encroachment by men of zeal, well-meaning but without understanding.

> Louis Brandeis
> *Olmstead* v. *United States*
> (1928)

The preceding chapters have described in some detail the effects on prices of the increasing federal presence in business management. While these effects are substantial and fairly immediate, there are other, less visible effects which may be more fundamental. The latter have to do with the changing locus of decision making and of responsibility for private sector activities.

The first "managerial revolution" was noted by Berle and Means more than four decades ago and given the title by James Burnham a decade later. These observers were referring to the divorce of the formal ownership of the modern corporation from the actual management.[1] A second managerial revolution is now under way—a silent bureaucratic revolution—in the course of which the locus of much of the decision making in the American corporation is shifting once

---

[1] "In the corporate system, the 'owner' of industrial wealth is left with a mere symbol of ownership while the power, the responsibility and the substance which have been an integral part of ownership in the past are being transferred to a separate group in whose hands lie control." A. A. Berle, Jr., and G. C. Means, *The Modern Corporation and Private Property* (New York: Macmillan, 1932), p. 68; see also James Burnham, *The Managerial Revolution* (Bloomington, Ind.: University Press, 1941).

again. This time the shift is from the professional management selected by the corporation's board of directors to the vast cadre of government regulators that influences and often controls the key decisions of the typical business firm. The added costs flowing from this change are ultimately borne by the public, in the form of higher taxes, higher prices, and lower real standards of living.

A Second Managerial Revolution

This revolution is neither deliberate nor socially disruptive. But a revolution it truly is—for it is forcing a fundamental change in the structure of our industrial society. The traditional concerns in business-government relations—Are we moving toward socialism? Are we in the grips of a military-industrial complex?—should be recognized as relevant to an age that has already passed.

Extending the analysis of Berle, Means and Burnham to the current situation, it is not who owns the means of production but who makes the key decisions that is crucial in determining the relative distribution of public and private power. Who exercises the major influence in deciding what lines of business a firm should go into? Which investments should it undertake? What products should it make? Under what conditions should they be produced? What prices should be charged?

The current trend, as has been noted in earlier chapters, is for the government to assume or at least share many of the key aspects of decision making of all firms. This is a silent revolution in many ways. It is not led by a host of noisy trumpeters. It is not intentional or even noticeable to the day-to-day observer. But that does not alter its deep impact.

The change that our industrial economy is undergoing must be understood as a bureaucratic revolution, not a conspiracy. What is involved are the lawful efforts of governmental civil servants going about their routine and assigned tasks, tasks whose purposes are hard to deny. Who, after all, is opposed to cleaning up the environment? Or enhancing job safety? Or improving consumer products?

Yet, if we step back and assess the long-term impact on the private enterprise system of the host of government inspections, regulations, reviews, and subsidies, we find that the fundamental business-government relationship is being changed. To be sure, the process is far from complete—and it proceeds unevenly—but the results to date are clear enough: increasingly the government is participating in and often controlling the internal decisions of business, the kinds of decisions that lie at the heart of the capitalist system.

As we said, it is a silent bureaucratic revolution, not conspiratorial and not intended to undermine the capitalist system. The men and women involved are sincerely attempting to carry out high priority national objectives which are considered basic to the quality of life in America.

Yet, those who have assigned the tasks, the Congress and the leadership of the executive branch, have failed to appreciate the enormous significance of their actions. If specific laws or regulations had been proposed for the government formally to take over private risk-bearing and initiative, the problem would have been faced head on, and the proposals probably defeated. And that of course is the crunch. This silent revolution is unintentional; it is an unexpected by-product—but a critically serious one—of the expanding role of government in our modern society. President Gerald Ford, who served in the House of Representatives for twenty-four years, has stated, "Most members of Congress don't realize the burdens that are placed upon business by the legislation they pass." [2]

As this study shows, the new types—and the infinite variety—of governmental regulations of business are not limited to the traditional regulatory agencies—the FTC, SEC, FPC, ICC, FCC, and so forth. Today the line departments and bureaus of government—the Departments of Agriculture, Commerce, HEW, Interior, Justice, Labor, Transportation, and Treasury—are deeply involved in actions that affect virtually every firm and most of its key operations. Governmental controls influence manufacturing, research and development, finance, personnel, marketing, facilities, and planning.

Let us take as a basic starting point the launching of a new business. In many cases, the prospective entrepreneur will find that entry is strictly controlled by a government agency. Examples vary from operating an airline or a radio or television station to distilling alcohol to manufacturing ethical drugs to producing nuclear materials.

Governmental regulation also extends to the introduction of new products into the marketplace. Clothing must now meet the requirements of the Wool Products Labeling Act. Drugs, of course, must be approved by the Food and Drug Administration. The administration of the Consumer Product Safety Act is just getting under way and its view of its charter appears to be extremely generous.

Governmental controls over the internal operating procedures of private companies also are expanding. As discussed earlier, govern-

---

[2] Juan Cameron, "Suppose There's a President Ford in Your Future," *Fortune*, March 1974, p. 206.

ment contractors must adhere to the pay and other standards of the Walsh-Healey Act, the Davis-Bacon Act, the Armed Services Procurement Act, and so forth. But far more employers are subject to laws governing minimum wages, overtime hours, equal pay, equal employment opportunity, and relations with unions. The often unwelcome federal inspector makes his appearances with increasing frequency and covers more facets of business activity each year.

No businessman today, whether the head of a large company or the corner grocer, can operate without considering a multitude of governmental restrictions and regulations. His or her costs and profits can be affected as much by a bill passed in Washington as by a management decision in the front office or a customer's decision at the checkout counter. The design and manufacture of the 1973 automobile, for example, was subject to forty-four government standards and regulations involving about 780 separate test points which must be met on each car. In the words of Richard C. Gerstenberg, chairman of the board of General Motors: "Government today has something to say about how we design our products, how we build them, how we test them, how we advertise them, how we sell them, how we warrant them, how we repair them, the compensation we pay our employees, and even the prices we may charge our customers." [3]

Virtually every major department of the typical industrial corporation in the United States has one or more counterparts in a federal agency that controls or strongly influences its internal decision making. As discussed before, the company's production department is aware of the presence of the Labor Department's occupational safety and health inspector. The marketing department must take account of the possibility of adverse rulings by the Consumer Product Safety Commission resulting in product recalls. The advertising department must respond to the government's efforts to shift the purpose of product packaging and labeling from sales promotion to safety and efficiency information. The personnel department must avoid running afoul of the equal employment opportunity regulations. The finance department must keep its books and financial reports so as to satisfy the Internal Revenue Service, the Securities and Exchange Commission, and governmentally sponsored credit agencies. The R&D department must work on products and processes that meet the requirements of the Environmental Protection Agency.

---

[3] General Motors Corporation, *1973 Report on Progress in Areas of Public Concern*, 1973, p. 88.

The Various Costs of Federal Regulation

In this day of rising attention to the costs as well as the benefits of public action, we must recognize the substantial costs that consumers pay for the truly massive expansion in government regulation of the private sector. These costs stem in part from the increased and unproductive overhead expenses that government requirements impose. They may not mean much to the taxpayer, but to the extent that they raise the cost of production, they result in higher prices to consumers. Because the government-mandated costs result in no measurable output, they also are reflected in the lower rate of productivity that has been experienced by the American economy in recent years.

John C. Whitehead of the investment banking firm of Goldman, Sachs and Company has measured the cost of one aspect of government regulation of business, the growing mass of financial information required by the SEC prior to its approval of a new securities issue. He reports that a foreign-based firm, a world famous public company, concluded that SEC requirements were so cumbersome that the company would raise its money elsewhere until there was at least a 1 percent annual interest differential in favor of issuing in the United States.[4]

Yet, the critical price we pay for government regulation is the attenuation of the risk bearing and entrepreneurial nature of our private enterprise system—a system which, at least in the past, has contributed so effectively to rapid rates of innovation, productivity, and growth. A hidden cost of governmental restrictions of various kinds is a reduced rate of innovation. The longer that it takes for some change to be approved by the federal regulatory agency—a new or improved product, a more efficient production process, et cetera—the less likely that the change will be made. In any event, innovation will be delayed.

Professor William Wardell of the University of Rochester's School of Medicine and Dentistry has studied in detail the advantages and disadvantages of Britain's liberal policy toward the introduction of new drugs. He concludes that, on balance, Great Britain gained in comparison with the United States from its more "permissive" policy toward the marketing of new drugs:

> . . . Britain suffered more toxicity due to new drugs than did the United States, as could have been anticipated from the fact that more new drugs were marketed there. How-

---

[4] John C. Whitehead, "SEC Must Drop Role of Industry Adversary," *Money Manager*, July 1, 1974, p. 21.

ever, considering the size of the total burden of drug toxicity, the portion due to new drugs was extremely small, and would in any case be at least partially offset by the adverse effects of older alternative drugs had the latter been used instead. Conversely, Britain experienced clearly discernible gains by introducing useful new drugs, either sooner than the United States or exclusively.[5]

Professor Sam Peltzman of the University of Chicago has estimated some of the costs of the drug lag in the United States. He analyzed the 1962 amendments to the food and drug act, amendments that were ostensibly designed to keep ineffective drugs off the market by extending the process of authorizing new drugs prior to their being available to the public. The main impact of the legislation has been to delay the introduction of effective drugs by about four years and to lead to higher prices for drugs. He estimates the resultant loss to the consumer to be in the neighborhood of $200-300 million a year. Peltzman also calculates that if the drugs that combat tuberculosis had been delayed by two years, the average delay now imposed by the Food and Drug Administration, the result would have been approximately 45,000 additional deaths.[6]

The adverse effect of regulation on innovation is likely to be felt more strongly by smaller firms than by the large companies. Thus it will have an anticompetitive impact. According to Dr. Mitchell Zavon, president of the American Association of Poison Control Centers:

> We've got to the point in regulatory action where it's become so costly and risky to bring out products that only the very largest firms can afford to engage in these risky ventures. To bring out a new pesticide you have to figure a cost of $7,000,000 and seven years of time.[7]

Federal regulation imposes other "costs" on the economy. The impact on the prospects for economic growth and productivity can be seen by examining some recent estimates of the size and composition of investment by manufacturing companies. Lewis Beman has estimated that, in real terms (after eliminating the effects of inflation),

---

[5] William M. Wardell, "Therapeutic Implications of the Drug Lag," *Clinical Pharmacology and Therapeutics*, vol. 15, no. 1 (January 1974), p. 73.

[6] Sam Peltzman, "An Evaluation of Consumer Protection Legislation: The 1962 Drug Amendments," *Journal of Political Economy*, September/October 1973, p. 1090; Sam Peltzman, *Regulation of Pharmaceutical Innovation* (Washington, D. C.: American Enterprise Institute, 1974).

[7] Sheila Rule, "Pesticide Regulations Called Too Stringent," *St. Louis Post-Dispatch*, September 18, 1974, p. 18F.

total capital spending by American manufacturing companies was no higher in 1973 than it was in 1969—about $26 billion in both years.

However, in 1973 a much larger proportion of capital spending was devoted to pollution and safety outlays than in 1969—$3 billion more. Hence, the effective additions to plant and equipment—the real investment in modernization and new capacity—were lower in 1973.[8] This helps to explain why the American economy, for a substantial part of 1973, appeared to lack needed productive capacity, despite what had been large annual investments in new plant and equipment in recent years.

These unproductive federally mandated costs are not all behind us. The House of Representatives recently passed the Energy Transportation Security Act, a measure which would require that 20 percent of all oil imports be carried in U.S.-flag vessels immediately and 30 percent after June 30, 1977. (The "protection" of the Jones Act, discussed in an earlier chapter, is limited to coast-wise shipping within the United States.) The House Merchant Marine Committee estimates that the higher transportation costs might add "a penny a gallon at most" to the price of gasoline. The Maritime Administration projects the added costs at two cents a gallon by 1985. With domestic consumption now at approximately 100 billion gallons a year, the proposed law would raise gasoline costs in the United States by about $1 billion a year now and at least $2 billion by 1985.[9]

In the guise of achieving equality in the treatment of men and women workers, a major effort is under way to shift an important and discretionary element of family costs to the society as a whole. The specific point at issue is whether companies should be required to pay disability benefits to employees on maternity leave. If the effort is successful, working women who become pregnant will receive sick pay for the period they are away from the job and also will be covered for the medical and hospitalization costs of childbirth.[10] These increased costs of course will show up in higher prices for the products and services sold by the companies involved. Thus, the average consumer will find that he or she is paying the pregnancy-related expenses of a large part of the population, including those of families who can pay these costs themselves.

---

[8] Lewis Beman, "Why Business Ran Out of Capacity," *Fortune*, May 1974, p. 262.

[9] "Cargo Preference Rules Might Boost Imported Oil Prices," *Industry Week*, June 24, 1974, p. 19; "Where Are You, Ralph Nader?" *Wall Street Journal*, July 30, 1974, p. 10.

[10] "Seeking Pay for Maternity Leave," *Business Week*, May 18, 1974, p. 74. A federal court in California has ruled that a state law denying unemployment benefits to a pregnant woman is unconstitutional.

The phenomenon described in this monograph is still in the process of development. Virtually all policy proposals affecting business are variations on the same theme: increase the scope and degree of governmental involvement while shifting costs from the federal treasury to the products and services that consumers buy. Restrictions on the use of land owned by private individuals are an obvious example which has received great congressional and public attention. Yet, more indicative of future policy may be the bill introduced by Senators Walter Mondale and Philip Hart in the first session of the 93d Congress (S. 2809, the National Employment Priorities Act). This bill would require, whenever possible, that employees and affected communities be given two-year advance notification of plant closings or relocations. It also would establish a National Employment Relocation Administration to investigate and report on the economic justification for plant shutdowns. If the closings were found to be "unjustified," investment tax credits would be withdrawn for up to ten years. Businesses also would receive technical and financial aid to forestall "unnecessary" closings. The possibility thus looms that in the future it literally may be impossible for a firm or a plant to go out of business, without at least some form of prior federal review.

Some understanding of what lies at the end of the course on which the nation has embarked can be gained by examining that sector of American industry which already relies, to a substantial degree, upon governmental leadership and assistance. In the last three decades, the major U.S. defense contractors have become accustomed to federal officials making the basic decisions on which products a firm shall produce, how it shall go about producing them, and how capital shall be provided—with the government, in the process, assuming a major portion of the risk and the role of the entrepreneur. More Lockheeds and General Dynamics—or more 1011s and TFXs (to cite the well-known products of the two large defense contractors most dependent on the government)—are surely not the route to a rising living standard or a reduced rate of inflation.

In its pioneering report on *Social Responsibilities of Business Corporations*, the Committee for Economic Development stated in 1971:

> The evidence clearly indicates that many of the goals of American society can best be realized by developing a system of incentives for private firms to do those social jobs which business can perform better and more economically than other institutions. Indeed, the entrepreneurial thrust of

business—if encouraged, guided, and carefully audited by government at all levels—may well be indispensable in achieving a permanent solution to the urban and other socio-economic problems that have badly overtaxed the capacity of public agencies.[11]

One basic incentive to which the federal government should give greater attention is the nurturing of an economic climate conducive to the high level of saving and investment necessary to finance a widening array of private sector undertakings. Given such a climate, federal involvement with many problems which, at least in the past, have been successfully handled in the private sector would become unnecessary.

This study is not intended to be a simple-minded attack on all forms of government control over industry. As a general proposition, a society—acting through its government—can and should take steps to protect consumers against rapacious sellers, individual workers against unscrupulous employers, and future generations against those who would waste the nation's basic resources. But, as in most things in life, sensible solutions are not matters of either/or, but rather of more or less. Thus, we may enthusiastically advocate stringent and costly government controls over industry to avoid infant crib deaths without simultaneously supporting a plethora of detailed federal rules and regulations which, as we have seen, deal with the size of toilet partitions, the color of exit lights, and the maintenance of cuspidors.

The Changing Structure of the Economy

In some areas of the economy, notably agriculture and shipping, the federal presence in internal business decision making is of long standing. In other areas, notably the civilian manufacturing industries, it is of quite recent origin. Table 19 is a preliminary effort to show the degree of federal control over different parts of the American economy.

Certainly, the government-business relationships being described in the table are not static. The motor vehicle manufacturing industry is currently experiencing a great expansion in federal regulation. In the case of the electric utilities, the traditional, relatively well-marked separation between the public and the private sectors is now in some danger of being eliminated or at least reduced. As shown in Chap-

---

[11] Committee for Economic Development, *Social Responsibilities of Business Corporations* (New York, 1971), p. 55.

Table 19

EXTENT OF GOVERNMENT CONTROLS, BY INDUSTRY

Industry	Partial Government Ownership	Government Dependence (subsidy)	Complete Government Control	Partial Government Control
Railroads	X	X	X	
Electric Utilities	X		X	
Agriculture		X		X
Shipping		X		X
Trade				X
Finance	X	X	X	
Services	X			X
Manufacturing:				
Defense	X	X	X	
Drugs			X	
Shipbuilding	X	X		X
Motor Vehicles				X
Other				X

ter 8, the financial difficulties facing many utilities are causing renewed interest in the possibility of federal assistance and control. It should be noted that the industry's financial difficulties result, in large measure, from shortcomings in state regulation.

It seems clear that the mixed economy now developing in the United States does not provide a clean dividing line between public and private functions. In the past, the term "mixed economy" has mainly meant that both public and private production of goods and services were being undertaken in the same industry. For example, the Tennessee Valley Authority and the Union Electric Company both generate and distribute electric power, the former being a government agency and the latter a private corporation. The Postal Service and the Railway Express Agency both deliver parcels; one is public and the other is private.

The new kind of mixed economy is different. It is characterized by mixed organizations that possess the characteristics of both public institutions and private agencies. Examples range from a major defense contractor, the Lockheed Aircraft Corporation, to a government-sponsored credit agency, the Federal National Mortgage Association. Both of these corporations are listed on the New York Stock Exchange and both are subject to substantial federal direction.[12] There is substantial federal capital in the former, while the stock in trade of the latter literally consists of assets whose value and earning power (such as FHA-guaranteed mortgages) are guaranteed by the federal government. As we have seen, both types of companies are instruments for carrying out national policy. In the case of a manufacturing company like Lockheed, its internal operations are also closely monitored by federal agencies.

Yet, some companies catering primarily to private markets—such as the drug or toy producers—find themselves increasingly subject to federal review and regulation in their own decision-making processes. Still other companies, notably the railroads, are seemingly on the brink of de facto nationalization. To a major extent, passenger rail service is now financed through the federally sponsored and subsidized National Railroad Passenger Corporation (popularly known as Amtrak). The federally owned U.S. Railway Association is now getting under way. To a substantial degree, the cost of this semi-nationalized business is already borne by the taxpayer.

With this turn of events, we no longer can employ usefully the old-fashioned notion that the degree to which a country is socialized is measured by the extent to which the means of production are publicly rather than privately owned. A second managerial revolution is unfolding, with government taking on a much larger and more pervasive role in the economy than has been traditional in this nation. The final section of the study attempts to present a forward-looking response to this new situation.

A New Approach to Business-Government Relations

By and large, the relationships between business and government in the United States can be described as basically adversary in nature. Government probes, inspects, taxes, influences, regulates, and punishes. At least that appears to be the dominant view in many quarters, in both the public and private sectors. In many ways, this unfavorable view comes uncomfortably close to reality.

There is a striking contrast between this situation (or at least this view of it) and what is often taken to be the dominant European and Japanese approach, where the relationship between business and government is seen as a "partnership" or at least close cooperation. Some have suggested that we import the "partnership" model con-

---

[12] See Murray L. Weidenbaum, *The Modern Public Sector* (New York: Basic Books, 1969), Chapter 8.

tending that the closer working relations this model implies would improve our competitive position abroad and enhance productivity at home. The difficulty is, however, that this approach could result in submerging the public, and especially the consumer, interest. Yet, the status quo is undesirable. It does not seem sensible to expect American business to wage a two-front war, struggling against increasing governmental encroachment at home and government-supported enterprises abroad.

There is a third approach, one which might be considered a variant of the foreign policy that is often called "peaceful coexistence." Thought should be given, in other words, to the possibility of making a sensible division of labor between the public and private sectors in achieving basic national objectives. In order to explore this possibility, first, a short summary—hopefully not a caricature—of the current method of deciding national priorities will be presented, with particular stress given to effects on business. Second, a new model of national decision making will be outlined.

In practice, government budget decisions, particularly on the spending side, are made in the small—in bits and pieces. The Congress acts on a great many individual authorization and appropriation bills. Then the separate items are added up, usually on a functional basis—so much for defense, a bit less for welfare, much less for education, et cetera. In this approach, business (if it is thought about at all) is regarded as an input, that is, one of a variety of tools or mechanisms that can be drawn upon. In the case of defense spending, business firms are very heavily utilized, although not always in an effective manner (see Chapter 6). In the case of the rapidly expanding income-maintenance programs, in contrast, business firms are hardly involved at all. Thus, a shift in emphasis in budget priorities from warfare to welfare, as has been occurring in recent years, means— perhaps altogether unwittingly—less emphasis on the direct utilization of business firms in carrying out national priorities. The earlier concern about moving toward a "contract state," in which key governmental responsibilities are delegated to private corporations, quite properly has faded away.

Another fiscal development has been occurring, however, which raises a quite different concern. The desire to exercise a greater degree of control over the size and growth of the federal budget—whether stemming from concern over the inflationary effects of budget deficits or the more philosophical resistance to the growth of the public sector—has led to efforts to "economize" on direct government spending by using government controls.

We need a fundamental rethinking of the tendency for government increasingly to regulate what essentially is internal business decision making. One model which could be followed is one where the process of determining national priorities would be viewed as a two-step affair. First, the Congress would focus, as it does to some extent today, on determining how much of our resources should be devoted to defense, welfare, education, and so forth. But, second, this determination would be accompanied by a general and tentative allocation of responsibilities among the major sectors of the economy. The rationale for this type of indicative planning would be the recognition that the constant and increasing nibbling away at business prerogatives and entrepreneurial characteristics has a very substantial cost—namely, reduced effectiveness in achieving some basic national objectives, notably (to use the language of the Full Employment Act) "maximum employment, production, and purchasing power." The proposed planning approach would also take account of the different mix of constituencies that the public and private sectors are primarily geared to serve.

In this day when benefit-cost analysis has become fashionable, we should not be oblivious of the very real if not generally measurable effects of converting ostensibly private organizations into involuntary agents of the federal establishment. Rather than pursuing the current course, the nation should determine which of its objectives can be achieved more effectively in the private than the public sector and go about creating an overall environment more conducive to the attainment of those objectives.

Without prejudging the results of such an examination, it would appear reasonable to expect that primarily social objectives—such as improved police services—would be the primary province of government. And primarily economic objectives—notably training, motivating, and usefully employing the bulk of the nation's work force—would be viewed as mainly a responsibility of the private sector, and especially of business firms.[13]

The new model of national decision making presented here hardly calls for an abdication of governmental concern with the substantive programs enumerated in earlier chapters. Rather, it would require a redirection of the methods selected for achieving essentially worthy ends. In the environmental area, for example, most of the current

---

[13] See Murray L. Weidenbaum, *A New Approach to Government-Business Relations: Peaceful Coexistence,* a paper prepared for the Conference on the Business-Government Relationship, University of California at Los Angeles, January 24, 1974.

direct controls would be scrapped in favor of the more indirect but powerful incentives available through the price system. Specifically, "sumptuary" excise taxation, which we have grown accustomed to in the cases of tobacco products and alcoholic beverages, can be used to alter basic production and consumption patterns.

The desired results in pollution abatement would not be accomplished by fiat, but rather by making the high-pollutant product or service more expensive relative to the low-pollutant product or service. Effluent fees encourage extensive efforts to reduce pollution by those who can do so at relatively low cost and lesser efforts by those for whom the costs would be greater. The objective, often overlooked, is not to punish polluters or to maximize the cost of ecological improvement, but to get a cleaner environment. The basic guiding principle would be that people and institutions do not pollute because they enjoy messing up the environment, but rather, because it is easier, cheaper, or more profitable to do so. A study of the Delaware estuary concluded that modest improvements in water quality might cost only half as much if accomplished by effluent fees as they would if accomplished through uniform controls over discharges.[14] Instead of a corps of inspectors or regulators, the price system should be used to make polluting more expensive and therefore less profitable.

There is a parallel here to the operation of a tariff system. Even a tariff instituted ostensibly only for revenue purposes keeps out some products—to the extent that demand and supply respond at all to price changes. And the higher the tariff, the closer it comes to becoming a "protective" tariff, keeping out the undesirable item entirely.

Other areas of the economy could benefit from using alternatives to governmental intervention in business operations. One such area, as we have seen, is the direction over the flow of saving and investment, a basic aspect of a capitalistic or other advanced economy. A result of the expanded use of governmentally sponsored credit agencies, such as the Federal Intermediate Credit Banks, the Export-Import Bank, and a host of others, is that a rising portion—as much as a third in recent years—of all the funds raised in ostensibly private capital markets in the United States now funnel through these federal financial intermediaries. In every period of credit tightness, there is a clamor for setting up additional ones—for example, an Aerospace Reconstruction Finance Corporation or an Energy Research and Development Corporation—in order to assure yet another category

---

[14] Allen V. Kneese and Blair T. Bower, *Managing Water Quality: Economics, Technology, Institutions* (Baltimore: Johns Hopkins Press, 1968), pp. 158-64.

of borrowers ready access to capital markets. Yet these federal instrumentalities do nothing to add to the available pool of investment funds. In practice, their creation and expansion amounts to robbing Peter to pay Paul. They also reduce the market's ability to allocate capital resources to the more efficient undertakings and result in the "unprotected" and truly private borrowers bidding up interest rates in order to obtain the funds they require. A more positive and fruitful approach to national policy in this area would be to create an overall economic environment which provides more incentive to individuals and business firms to save and thus to generate more investment funds available to the society as a whole.

In the OSHA area the law has lost sight of the basic objective—to achieve a safer working environment. Instead, the current emphasis is on punishing violations. In the more positive spirit of the approach suggested here, the basic emphasis of the occupational safety and health legislation would be shifted from enumerating specific practices to be followed in a company's operations to reducing its accident and health hazard rate. It is doubtful that there is an invariant, unique way of achieving that desirable result. Changes in equipment, variations in working practices, education and training of employees, and leadership on the part of management all may be practical alternatives for achieving the desired ends, at least in some circumstances. An economist would opt for the mix of methods which entails the least loss of productivity and output, and those combinations would probably vary from plant to plant and over time.

It should be recognized that the results of such decentralized decision making may not necessarily coincide with those of a more centralized system. We would undoubtedly have different mixes of goods and services under the two approaches. That implicit reordering of priorities may be the real price we have to pay for reducing centralized control. Yet, the reordering of priorities may only happen in a relative sense. If our nation's resources are utilized more effectively as a result of reducing the costly burden of government controls and influence, the increased national output could yield perhaps the same or even more of the new lower priority items (in absolute terms). In any event, the total level of economic welfare should be enhanced—or, at the minimum, we would have a greater opportunity for enhancing it as a result of the increased efficiency and productivity that could be anticipated—and in a less inflationary environment.

A new division of labor between public and private undertakings should not be expected to remain constant over time. Rather, it should be expected to change—with underlying circumstances, foreign and domestic, and with the experience gained from following a strategy of peaceful coexistence between business and government in the United States. Hopefully, that dividing line between public and private responsibilities would shift back and forth, rather than in a predictable single direction as it has in the past.

SELECTED 1974 PUBLICATIONS TO DATE

NATIONAL ENERGY STUDIES

U.S. ENERGY POLICY: A PRIMER, Edward J. Mitchell *(103 pages, $3.00)*

NATURAL GAS REGULATION: AN EVALUATION OF FPC PRICE CONTROLS, Robert B. Helms *(84 pages, $3.00)*

ENERGY SELF-SUFFICIENCY: AN ECONOMIC EVALUATION, M.I.T. Energy Laboratory Policy Study Group *(89 pages, $3.00)*

DIALOGUE ON WORLD OIL: HIGHLIGHTS OF A CONFERENCE ON WORLD OIL PROBLEMS (32 pages, $1.00)

DIALOGUE ON WORLD OIL, edited by Edward J. Mitchell *(106 pages, paper $3.00, cloth $6.50)*

THE NATURAL GAS SHORTAGE AND THE CONGRESS, Patricia E. Starratt *(68 pages, $3.00)*

PERFORMANCE OF THE FEDERAL ENERGY OFFICE, Richard B. Mancke *(25 pages, $1.50)*

OTHER STUDIES AND PROCEEDINGS

ARMS IN THE PERSIAN GULF, Dale R. Tahtinen *(31 pages, $2.00)*

THE ENERGY CRISIS, Paul W. McCracken, moderator *(110 pages, $2.00)*

PRIVATE FOUNDATIONS: BEFORE AND AFTER THE TAX REFORM ACT OF 1969, William H. Smith and Carolyn P. Chiechi *(83 pages, $3.00)*

REGULATION OF PHARMACEUTICAL INNOVATION: THE 1962 AMENDMENTS, Sam Peltzman *(118 pages, $3.00)*

FEDERAL TRANSIT SUBSIDIES: THE URBAN MASS TRANSPORTATION ASSISTANCE PROGRAM, George W. Hilton *(131 pages, $3.00)*

SIGNIFICANT DECISIONS OF THE SUPREME COURT, 1972-73 TERM, Bruce E. Fein *(136 pages, $3.00)*

THE FUTURE OF THE CHINA MARKET: PROSPECTS FOR SINO-AMERICAN TRADE, Edward Neilan and Charles R. Smith *(94 pages, $3.00)*

AGREEMENT ON BERLIN: A STUDY OF THE 1970-72 QUADRIPARTITE NEGOTIATIONS, Dennis L. Bark *(131 pages, $3.00)*

FOOD SAFETY REGULATION: A STUDY OF THE USE AND LIMITATIONS OF COST-BENEFIT ANALYSIS, Rita Ricardo Campbell *(59 pages, $3.00)*

ESSAYS ON INFLATION AND INDEXATION, Herbert Giersch, Milton Friedman, William Fellner, Edward M. Bernstein, Alexandre Kafka *(98 pages, $3.00)*

RESPONSIBLE PARENTHOOD: THE POLITICS OF MEXICO'S NEW POPULATION POLICIES, Frederick C. Turner *(43 pages, $2.00)*

THE HYDRA-HEADED MONSTER: THE PROBLEM OF INFLATION IN THE UNITED STATES, Phillip Cagan *(59 pages, $3.00)*

IS THE ENERGY CRISIS CONTRIVED? Paul W. McCracken, moderator *(44 pages, $2.00)*

INFLATION AND THE EARNING POWER OF DEPRECIABLE ASSETS, Eric Schiff *(36 pages, $2.00)*

WHAT PRICE DEFENSE?, Edmund S. Muskie and Bill Brock *(73 pages, paper $2.50, cloth $5.75)*

TOWARD A REALISTIC MILITARY ASSISTANCE PROGRAM, Robert J. Pranger and Dale R. Tahtinen *(48 pages, $2.00)*

BRAZIL AND THE UNITED STATES: TOWARD A MATURING RELATIONSHIP, Roger W. Fontaine *(127 pages, $3.00)*

OBSCENITY: THE COURT, THE CONGRESS AND THE PRESIDENT'S COMMISSION, Lane V. Sunderland *(127 pages, $3.00)*

Government-Mandated Price Increases: A Neglected Aspect of Inflation by Murray L. Weidenbaum takes a look at government policies which, however inadvertently, impose higher costs on private business and, thereby, raise consumer prices.

In recent years, partly in an attempt to achieve national objectives without spending large amounts of public funds, government has increasingly resorted to a practice that, in effect, transfers public requirements to the private sector. Thus, for example, instead of the public treasury's bearing the full burden of cleaning up the environment or improving highway safety, private decision makers are influenced or required to foot the bill. Weidenbaum notes that the imposition of "socially desirable" requirements on business looks like an inexpensive way to fulfill national objectives: it costs the government almost nothing and therefore seems to add little to the taxpayers' burden. But, he asks, does the nation really get a "free lunch"?

The author examines the effects of this practice in the fields of automobile production, consumer products, government procurements, personnel, and interest rates, among others. He concludes that while the objectives of increasing government regulation may be worthy, the costs show up in higher prices for goods and services—a "hidden tax" that has simply been shifted from taxpayer to consumer.

Murray L. Weidenbaum is director of the Center for the Study of American Business at Washington University in St. Louis, Missouri, and an adjunct scholar at the American Enterprise Institute. From 1969 to 1971, he served as assistant secretary of the Treasury for economic policy.

$3.00

 American Enterprise Institute for Public Policy Research
1150 Seventeenth Street, N.W., Washington, D. C. 20036

8016